D1441431

Dick Spady:
A LIFE OF VISIONS AND VALUES

RICHARD SPADY,
AS TOLD TO KATHLEEN L. O'CONNOR

ISBN: 0615953832
ISBN-13: 9780615953830

Acknowledgments

*T*hank you to Kathleen O'Connor, a writer living and working in Seattle, whom I commissioned to write my father's story. Thanks also to Nancy Rudy, copy editor.

And special thanks to my family reviewers: my mother and father, my wife Tatyana, and my brothers Jim, Walt, and Doug.
-John Spady

And finally, on behalf of my father and our family, a very special acknowledgment to *Dick's* customers:

When I hear someone say, "Dick's Drive-Ins are like a member of the family," it says to me that our sense of community is healthy and strong. We now have three generations (going on four!) of Spadys who have come of age within the family business, and I could not have picked a better or more vibrant community to build a family heritage. To the greater Seattle and Edmonds communities, thank you for being part of our family. You have showered us with praise and awards, and it is our hope that we have, in good measure, returned the goodwill you have extended to us.

Dick Spady, January 2014

TABLE OF CONTENTS

Chapter One: Dick's Early Years 1

Chapter Two: The Road to *Dick's* 21

Chapter Three: The Stores and More 29

Chapter Four: Propelled by Values, Vision and Voice . . 71

Chapter Five: A Word that Changed a Life and
                 Fostered a New Body of Research 85

Chapter Six: A Voice for the Vision. 99

Chapter Seven: Family Life. 117

Appendices 131
   1. Dick's Philosophy of Business
   2. Dick's Employee Benefits
   3. Red and Rover: Brian Bassett Comic Strip
   4. Senate Resolution 1993-8636
   5. Honorary Doctorate
   6. Awards and Honors
   7. Mayor's Proclamation

Chapter 1

DICK'S EARLY YEARS

*L*ittle did Dick dream, as he was whipping up ice cream in a cold-storage locker a heartbeat from the equator during World War II, that he would end up founding one of Seattle's most beloved eateries. Nor could he ever have imagined, as a four-year-old child living with his grandmother right before the onset of the Great Depression, that one day he would have four sons and a daughter of his own who would be raised in a home on a lake.

Nor did he dream, when he was cleaning his former elementary school at age seventeen, that one day he would own a business that carried his own name.

Nor would he ever have imagined that one word could change a life.

When we enter this world, none of us knows where the roads will take us, but they often make sense looking back. Dick was born on October 15, 1923, six years before the stock market crash of 1929 and the beginning of the Great Depression. He spent his early years in Portland, Oregon, but when his parents divorced, he lived with his grandmother Goldie (Pringle) Ewen Van Wart whose farm was near what is now Tigard, Oregon. He rejoined his mother in Portland after she married Raymond Schmeer in 1928. Dick Spady then became Dick Schmeer.

Dick had three grandmothers—Van Wart, Schmeer, and Spady. His Grandmother Schmeer even lived along the walk to his high school, so Dick had many eyes watching out for him.

He was raised essentially as an only child, given the age difference between him and his two stepbrothers—Norman Schmeer (1933–2013), who was 10 years younger, and Greg Schmeer (1948–), who was 25 years younger. Despite the differences in their ages, he and his brothers remained close.

Dick was an enterprising child and young man, a trait no doubt fostered by the Depression. Ever resourceful at age nine, he found a job sweeping a small family-owned grocery store once a week. That job, as it turns out, would help shape his future. The job paid a dime a week, which enabled him to go into town and see a movie—tickets then were a nickel. Being frugal, he saved the other nickel and finally put away enough money to buy his first treat—an Emerson radio.

In elementary school, he took on a paper route with the *Oregon Journal*, which he kept for three years. His territory was so large that when he left, the *Journal* split it into two routes. In his last year of high school, he found a new job—this time inside—cleaning the bathrooms and hallways of his own former elementary school, Beaumont Grammar School.

Despite going to school and working, Dick found time for sports. He began playing softball in elementary school and kept playing through high school. He was in a park league, and the teams literally grew up together: first, for players 4'2", then 4'4", then 4'8", and finally unlimited. His team played well all the way from the first through the unlimited divisions, and the teams continued to play well into the war when Dick left.

Dick had also worked with trains earlier at *St. John's Junction* in north Portland while he was in high school. He was not a paid employee, but the chief dispatcher had authorized him to be there. He learned to take care of the critical "Y" switch that sent trains in two different directions—one to the south and the other to the north through a tunnel. It gave him the opportunity to receive some real experience. Three men assigned to the junction befriended him and encouraged his learning.

Because college was not an affordable option for Dick at the time, he began thinking about the kind of work he wanted to do when he finished high school. After some thought, he decided to explore telegraphy—the art of sending telegraphic, Morse code messages. Dick enrolled in evening courses on the subject and studied once a week for over two years. Under the tutelage of Lem Devers, he began practicing the clicking "dots" and "dashes" of Morse code. His frequent practice enabled him to master telegraphy so well that when Dick graduated from high school in January 1941, he was hired on as a telegrapher by the Union Pacific Railroad and was assigned to the "extra board," which meant he replaced the regular operators when they were sick or on vacation.

His first major assignment was 20 miles west of Portland in the small town of Quinton, Oregon, on the Columbia River. The section foreman and his wife took care of his meals. A small café a half-mile east of the station had a little playhouse with a bunk bed. So, with this bunk bed in an eight-foot-by-eight-foot building, he now had food and also a place to sleep. Being new to the post, he was assigned the night shift.

Dick was hardly there two weeks when the chief dispatcher asked him to work in Portland at the East Portland Interlocking Plant. After a month of training, he became the relief operator for the entire plant at the east end of what is now the Steel Bridge where the Portland Train Depot is located. In this post, Dick was responsible for controlling the 99 different plant levers directing all the trains. He is convinced the only reason he got the job was because of all the studying he had done and the earlier learning he was given to understand train switches.

Working at the East Portland Interlocking Plant filled Dick with excitement and pride—here he was at age 18 receiving a full union wage. He was earning as much money pay as someone who had worked for the railroads for 30 years. And, as Dick is fond of reminding everyone, he was working with real trains, not toys. Heady times for a young man fresh out of high school!

Like all young men at that time, Dick registered with the draft. His induction was deferred, however, because he worked for the railroad. Railroads were considered to be part of the defense industry because of their critical role in shipping military products, goods, and personnel. Dick worked with Union Pacific from 1941 until he eventually shipped out with the Navy as a Seabee in 1943, at the height of World War II combat in the Pacific.

Registering for a Social Security card to work on the Union Pacific, however, changed Richard "Schmeer" back into Richard "Spady." Dick's stepfather had never formally or legally adopted him or changed his name to Schmeer. Lacking any formal documents, the Social Security administration assigned him his original birth name – Spady. From the age of five to 19, he was Dick Schmeer; consequently, there are no records of the name Dick Spady from his early school days, nor any information on him in official sources, including the U.S. Census.

In September 1943, when he was finally inducted, Dick was asked if he wanted to serve in the Army or the Navy. Stunned that he had a choice, he immediately chose the Navy because he thought he would at least have a bed. Dick was inducted but could not serve in combat because he wore glasses and could not see well enough to shoot. He was shipped off instead to the Seabees Construction Battalion at Espirito Santo island in the New Hebrides (part of an archipelago in what is now the Republic of Vanuatu in the South Pacific)—then a joint British-French protectorate just off the equator. Dick felt like a sitting duck as he was shipped out to the New Hebrides on one of three unescorted Liberty ships at the height of the Pacific war. But they arrived safely, and he was assigned to dig ditches. The New Hebrides were important to the success of the war in the Pacific.

World War II turned out to be pivotal in Dick's career—it offered him the experience he would need to start and manage a business. It also gave him the GI Bill, which meant he could go to college after the war, a dream previously out of reach.

One day, after he had spent several weeks digging ditches, naval officers asked the troops if anyone had experience working in a grocery store. Remembering his work at age nine sweeping the grocery store floor, Dick immediately raised his hand.

He was then assigned to work in small stores that managed the clothing of the battalion. Three men were assigned to the unit—one was a first class petty officer, another was a third class petty officer, and the third was Dick, a seaman. The unit soon had an added responsibility—making ice cream for the battalion. Being the lowest-ranking member of the team, Dick made the ice cream.

Because they were in the hot and humid tropics, making ice cream was a challenge. On the day he made ice cream each week, he spent two hours in the 10-degree cold-storage freezer whipping ice cream mix. So, ironically, Dick's experience with ice cream started in the tropics.

After six months, he was shipped to Iroquois Point at Pearl Harbor in Hawaii. He was assigned to the ABCD (Advanced Base Construction Depot) of the Seabees, where he was responsible for receiving and issuing supplies.

DICK'S EARLY YEARS

Hawaii was where Dick met H. Warren Ghormley (Ghorm), who would later become his business partner at *Dick's* Drive-In Restaurants. After six months, Dick was shipped off to Guam. There, he had a similar assignment, which lasted until the end of the war, when he was honorably discharged.

Armed with the GI Bill after the war, Dick could fulfill his dream of gaining a college education. He enrolled in Oregon State University (OSU) in Corvallis and majored in business and technology. He had to choose an emphasis in business. Rather than choosing accounting or finance, Dick picked "production." He also had to choose a minor, so he selected physics. After one term, however, he realized that while he had learned a lot about light and sound, it wasn't the field for him. He transferred out of physics and chose building construction in the architecture school instead. He figured everyone needed a home, so he thought he should learn about it.

Still wanting to give something back to his country while at OSU in 1947, Dick enrolled in the Air Force ROTC. In his first term, he was made cadet commander because his grades were so high. He later became a second lieutenant in the active reserves during his senior year. At graduation, he received the "Distinguished Military Graduate" award, which carried an invitation to join the regular Air Force for a career, similar to the invitation to the graduates of the Air Force Academy.

After graduating from college in 1950, Dick didn't have the money he needed to start his own business, which had been his long-standing dream. He wanted to be involved in real estate and finance and found work with Milo K. McIver, at the Commerce Investment Company, for $300 per month. The Commerce Investment Company specialized in the construction of inexpensive homes, but, as Dick said, while they were small homes, they were well constructed. Dick was in sales. His job was also to sell land, and he was the only person in the company who did so.

Dick worked for McIver about a year before his reserve unit was activated to serve in the Korean War in 1951. This second military experience would be as important as the first in terms of providing him with the skills he would need to open and manage *Dick's*.

Because Dick had enrolled in Advanced Air Force ROTC at OSU, he was in the active reserves. When the Korean War started, Dick was called up into the 403rd Troop Carrier Wing, under the command of General McCarty. Because Dick had a business degree, he was assigned to be the commissary officer and was responsible for storing and issuing rations for the wing. At the time, the wing consisted of 1,000 men based in Portland.

Commissary officers are "accountable" officers who are financially liable for their work. A few other officers are also accountable officers, such as the base supply and post exchange officers. While Dick did not have a real commissary store to manage at the 403rd Wing, he was responsible for issuing food for troop meals and for retirees who could obtain food at the Air Force facilities.

Because the Air Force provisions were then obtained from the Army, the menu for the wing came from the quartermaster of the Army and the Army's "master menu." The Army created menus months in advance so the commissary officers could plan ahead and have time to order the necessary food and supplies. They knew well in advance which meals would be served on any given day. Each menu was designed to serve 100 men.

The commissary officer was required to send in monthly reports. Every report had to adhere to very strict rules. Commissary officers could not make a "profit" of more than 5 percent; nor could they have losses of more than 5 percent of the cost of the rations. Dick closed the books at the end of the first month at his new post and wrote his report. When he was finished, his report showed a loss of more than $2,000, for which he could be held personally liable! At first he thought he had issued more food than he should have.

Worried, Dick went over the report again. He thought he had completed it correctly the first time, but as he started recalculating, he realized there was something wrong with the basic formula and the regulations.

For example, his report stipulated that the commissary officer was basically allowed to spend a total of $1 a day per person for breakfast, lunch, and dinner. The 1,000 men in the wing, however, were largely living off base. This meant that while most of the men were eating breakfast and dinner at home—the most expensive of the meals—they were all eating lunch on the base. Dick calculated a list of what it would cost to feed one airman one ration for one day.

Dick figured that if each meal were prepared for a cost of 33 cents per day per airman, then it did not matter if a different number of troops ate at breakfast, lunch or dinner. But if the same number of troops did not come to each meal, there would be different numbers at each meal, and that would cause distortions in the report.

Dick decided he had two choices: he could either change the menu and substitute inexpensive items so he could balance the books, or he could give the troops the nutritious food they deserved, according to the master menu, and exceed the amount authorized to be issued.

Dick was concerned enough about the formula's flaws that he prepared a report explaining the distortions and took it to the lieutenant colonel who was the commander of the supply squadron. He in turn sent Dick to the group commander who sent him to the general.

Dick was a second lieutenant at the time—not the lowest person on the totem pole, but pretty far down the chain of command. The next lower position was not an officer.

Dick's report said he had two conflicting regulations—follow the master menu at 33 cents each per meal and follow the budget, which in order to do, he would have to change the menu and its meals with distortions—or he could substitute less expensive food that would look good on the report but would not be nutritious. The general was in a position to say yes or no. He supported Dick's report and sent it to headquarters.

Dick never heard back from the higher command on his report. So he sent in the same report the second month and again on the third month. He heard nothing back each time, even though he reported he was over issue by $2,000 each month.

On his 91st day on the job, Dick received orders to report to Itazuki Air Force Base in Southern Japan. He was the only one in the Portland Wing to receive such orders. He was sent orders by the 8th Air Force in Japan, and he served a year at Itazuki Air Force Base from 1951 to 1952. Dick was now responsible for serving thousands of active-duty troops.

He was sent to Itazuki because the Air Force needed a replacement for their commissary officer, a captain, who was being transferred. The commissary officer's job was largely to store and issue supplies to base dining halls and to account for those supplies. The Commissary Officer Central Office and the warehouses supplied groceries for over 400 families on the base and 10,000 troops in the field.

As the incoming commissary officer, Dick and his staff counted every case and its contents. The outgoing officer also had a team to do his outgoing inventory. Then the two groups reconciled their respective reports.

For example, if there were 50 cases by Dick's count and the other officer had a different number, they would have to recount that inventory. When all this was completed, the commissary officer submitted the report. Because Dick was replacing a commissary officer, the inventory was completed by both of them in a joint report.

Three days into his new assignment, a staff sergeant sent as an auditor by the 8th Air Force Command came to him and reported that he had completed an audit of the outgoing commissary officer and found a full page of discrepancies between the "issue" slips from the warehouse and delivery slips to the dining hall.

The sergeant told Dick the account was "unfit" for audit extending over the past six months. Buying time, Dick asked the sergeant to go back and double-check. Dick then called the supply officer immediately to inform him and suggested the supply officer contact the group commander about the discrepancies so he would know what was coming and would not be caught by surprise.

Two days later, the sergeant had two new pages of discrepancies. Dick called the squadron commander and asked him if he knew that the sergeant was planning on going directly to the wing commander about the audit. The group commander did not know about the audit and had not been called.

That same week, the group commander called Dick, saying, "Report to my office on Monday morning and tell me what the problem is and what you are going to do about it."

Three days later, the inspector general of the 8th Air Force, a lieutenant colonel, called Dick and said, "You don't have to be in balance the first month or the second month, but if you can't fix this by the third month, you've had it."

The audit had found a $6-million discrepancy. Dick, a second lieutenant on his first major assignment, had days to discover the problem and 90 days to fix it.

Meanwhile, the inspector general created a board to oversee reconciling discrepancies between issuing and receiving documents. The board used a balance sheet to document which supplies had been issued by the commissary and how many had been received by the dining hall. The inspector general also specified that Dick was *not* to serve on the board because he had the operational responsibility for the commissary.

Dick discovered the problem was in the warehouse "bin" cards. Each bin or crate that held the supplies had a pocket on the outside listing the contents inside. When someone removed something, the withdrawal was marked on the bin card; if something was restocked, that was also listed on the "bin" card.

The problem was, however, that everyone in the warehouses had access to the bin cards. If the content and bin card did not match at the end of the day, it was easy to change the bin card to make the numbers match. Anyone could do it. So, if the bin card said there were 100 cans at the end of the day, when 90 were actually in the bin, it was easy to just change the number to 90.

Dick thought, "*If you take away the bin card, no one in the warehouses will know what is in the supply box.*"

On the other hand, the commissary office personnel, who knew the correct totals, didn't handle the supplies. The simple change of having the commissary personnel control the bin cards could solve the problem and thus bring both control and accountability to commissary management.

Because there had been inventory discrepancies, Dick asked his staff sergeant responsible for the warehouses to recount the beef boneless in 20-pound boxes. When he asked the sergeant if he had recounted, the sergeant said, "Yes, it was all there." But the sergeant had not actually recounted the beef, and there were still discrepancies. The warehouse sergeant was relieved of duty by Dick, and Dick was assigned a new second lieutenant to oversee the commissary office warehouses.

Making the change in the management of the bin cards enabled Dick to balance the inventory the first month, the second month, and the third month. Months later, Dick learned the captain who had been the former commissary officer had been decommissioned and demoted to sergeant.

This experience led Dick to the first tenet in what would become his Philosophy of Business: *"Never make reality conform to paperwork. Always make paperwork conform to reality."*

Chapter 2

THE ROAD TO DICK'S

*B*ack from the war and eager to make a career, Dick returned to work in 1952 with Milo McIver at the Commerce Investment Company and its McKell Homes. Dick had always wanted to work in real estate and finance. This position gave him that opportunity.

One day, Dick went to lunch at a little café in southwest Portland called The Carnival. It had both tables and a lunch counter. He sat down at the counter directly in front of a household refrigerator. When the waiter opened the refrigerator door, Dick was amazed to see all the stacks of hamburger patties—they filled the entire refrigerator from top to bottom.

"How many days does it take you to sell all those hamburgers?" Dick asked.

"Days?" The waiter laughed. "We go through this one and two more like it in the back each day."

"That adds up," Dick thought to himself. Then he did the math and went to work drafting a 17-page business plan, which he sent off to his friend and former fellow Seabee, Ghorm, in Seattle. Ghorm had finished college as well and was working as an underwriter at Safeco Insurance Company.

Dick proposed that they should open a restaurant in Seattle because it had more zip than Portland. Dick was not thinking fast food, just a hot little restaurant like The Carnival.

Ghorm read the business plan and wrote back, "Okay, let's do it!" They formed their partnership in 1953, together with Dr. B. O. A. ("Tom") Thomas, DDS, who was a non-working partner, and they all continued as partners until August 1991, when Dick bought out Ghorm and Tom. Dick had expected to go into business only with Ghorm. He did not expect the advent of another partner, who turned out to be an important addition, providing both credit resources and counseling.

Ghorm's wife worked at the School of Dentistry at the University of Washington as the secretary for Dr. Thomas who had a Ph.D. in dentistry, periodontics, and anatomy. He was also the first Chair of the Department of Periodontology at the University. When she told him her husband was going into the hamburger business, he found that interesting. He was a member of the University Congregational Church Board of Trustees, and just the week before, one of the church's board members, who was the assistant sales manager of Carnation Dairy Company, told the board members about this new concept in California called "fast food." Restaurants were selling hamburgers for 19 cents, milkshakes for 21 cents, and French fries for 11 cents. "They're knocking them dead down there," he said.

With the help of Carnation, Dick and Ghorm decided to go to California to check it out. In California, they met Jim Collins, who owned one of the stores and showed them around. They even paid Collins $50 to let them work at the restaurant for a couple of hours so they could learn the ropes. Collins would later become president of the *Collins Foods International Corporation* and (among other things) own all the KFC franchises in Oregon, Washington, and California.

On the trip home, Dick wrote up a business plan to see where the financial break-even point would be. The new restaurant concept was working in California, but would it work in the Northwest where there were not as many people and it rained all the time? They could do the numbers, but would it work in Seattle?

Still, they decided to give it a try. In September 1953, Dick moved to Seattle. Dr. Thomas came on as a partner. Each of the partners put up an equal sum of $5,000. Dick borrowed some money from his uncle George, but he was still short. Dick had told Jim Gauld, his sales manager at Commerce that he was quitting to start a restaurant in Seattle. Dick knew that he had money coming from his sales commissions, but he was not sure how much. He still needed $3,000 in addition to the $800 he had borrowed from his uncle. He gathered his courage and asked Gauld to loan him $3,000 so he could get started. Gauld agreed. They went to the bank and obtained a loan with Gauld's stock as security. Dick would remain friends with Gauld and his wife throughout his life.

With money now in hand, they had to decide where to start and where to locate their store. Dick immediately began to study traffic flows in pre-freeway Seattle. They looked at several pieces of land and decided on a lot in Wallingford—111 Northeast 45th Street—about one mile west of the University of Washington and close to Lincoln High School.

The site was vacant at the time. It was 100 feet deep, 200 feet wide, and on the south side of the street. They were able to acquire a ground lease, but the owner would not sell or mortgage the land. This presented a problem. No one would build on property someone else owned.

Dick and Ghorm couldn't find the money they needed anywhere to build on the lot. They tried to use their GI Bill loans but were refused because it was too risky. They were getting turned down everywhere. Then Dick had an idea. He thought he might be able to get a contractor to split the cost of construction with Dr. Thomas and participate in the profits for the first five years at a guaranteed minimum market rate.

Dick went to the Seattle Builders' Association and laid out the issues they faced and asked if they knew anyone who would be interested in building under these conditions. They referred him to a contractor whose father had recently died and who had an engineering degree from the University of Washington. Dick arranged a meeting with him and pitched the idea.

A couple of weeks later, Dick went back to meet with him to learn his decision. *"We have no other irons in the fire. If this doesn't work, we won't have a restaurant,"* Dick thought.

Heart in hand, he met with the contractor. When the conversation started, the contractor said, "My banker and attorney don't like it. My accountant says, it won't work. My insurance broker says it's too risky." Dick's heart skipped a beat after each statement.

"But if I did everything those guys told me to do," he continued, "I'd be working for them in six months. We're good to go."

One of the reasons this arrangement worked is that the contractor's business (Sellen) was primarily in Alaska, so he and his crew could not work in the fall and winter. But by building the drive-in, he could keep his foreman, Bill McKinstry, (who was based in Seattle) busy during the winter.

The drive-in had to have an easy, friendly name. They thought of calling it Tom's, but Dr. Thomas said no. Then one day, Ghorm and Dr. Thomas told Dick they thought it should be called *Dick's,* and so it was.

Dick's on 45th opened on January 28, 1954. And the rest, as they say, is history. But it was not always a straight trajectory.

Because *Dick's* opened on January 28, they did not close the books in January and kept them opened through February. They closed the books at the end of February and breathlessly turned the financials over to their accountant. They anxiously awaited his analysis. When the accountant finished reviewing the balance sheet, he smiled and said, "I think it is going to fly with its own wings."

The Wallingford *Dick's* was profitable the first month, the second month, and the third month. It was working.

Opening day, however, prompted their first menu decision. The first *Dick's* only sold hamburgers, cheeseburgers with mustard and ketchup, fries, shakes, and some soft drinks. On opening day, however, both the hamburgers and cheeseburgers had chopped onions as part of the original recipe. Looking at the sticky, gooey, mushy restaurant floor at the end of that first day, Ghorm and Dick quickly decided, "*No onions! But, if the customer wants onions, we can give them to our customers in a small cup.*"

Their next major policy decision: "It's making money. Should we build more restaurants or franchise?" Franchise meant travel, and Dick and Ghorm wanted to raise families, not be off traveling to franchises. "*We did not franchise. We wanted to bloom where we were planted,*" Dick remembers.

Their second store opened a year later in January 1955. But unlike 45th, the Broadway store did not fly on its own wings right away. *Dick's* might have folded if it had not been for an unforeseen development about half a block north at Ivar's.

Chapter 3

THE STORES AND MORE

THE STORES

*D*ick's site in Wallingford was in a perfect location — near the University of Washington and between two rival high schools — Roosevelt and Lincoln, although closer to Lincoln. Prices were right for a young crowd, and *Dick's* became popular very quickly. Parking was ample, and it was on several major bus lines. *Dick's* immediately bloomed.

When *Dick's* opened in 1954, it was about nine years after the end of World War II and six months after the end of the Korean War. America was thriving. The austerity of the war years was gone and the Great Depression was a fading memory.

Peace and prosperity were returning to the country. More people could afford cars and more people were eating out. The food industry was changing. Fast food restaurants where people "dined" in their cars were ripe for the times. "Multi-mix" Milkshake machines were coming on the market for the first time, making it possible to quickly produce a quality product. All in all, a heady time in the restaurant and food business.

Dick and Ghorm's goal, however, was not just to serve fast food. Their goal was to serve delicious, nutritious, high-quality food quickly and inexpensively. They wanted consistent quality so that the customers' expectations were always met and they experienced the same taste, smells and texture each and every time they came.

Dick and Ghorm also agreed that they would never act unless both of them agreed on a course of action. If one of them disagreed, they would not act. It took both to chart a new course of action or to make a major business decision—a philosophy that continues to this day in a slightly different form. With a new business structure in place after 1991, final decisions are made by Dick, who as a cofounder and namesake, remains "president for life."

When *Dick's* opened, they sold milkshakes—chocolate, vanilla, and strawberry—hamburgers, cheeseburgers, coffee, and sodas. There was a separate window for fries and another for everything else.

The novelty of *Dick's* Drive-In Restaurants, the quality of its food, its low prices, and its accessibility made it a big hit. Its reputation grew by word of mouth. In fact, the only advertising they did originally for *Dick's* was in the university and high school newspapers—the perfect market. Hamburgers were 19 cents, milkshakes were 21 cents, and fries 11 cents. It was tasty food that almost everyone, especially high school and university students, could afford.

Dick's even survived its first disaster—a rare, full-blown Seattle blizzard in February 1954, which closed them for a few days, not long after they opened. But when the snow was gone, the customers returned. Having decided not to franchise, but instead to "*bloom where we were planted*," Dick, Ghorm, and Tom began thinking of expanding.

Heady with success, they chose Broadway for their next store. They picked a spot just a couple of blocks north of Broadway High School (now Seattle

Central Community College) and half a block from the Broadway movie theater (now a RiteAid pharmacy). Broadway *Dick's* opened in January 1955, a year after their first store. But things did not start out so well for them this time.

The site was different. The 100 ft- by 120-ft parking lot was not as open or accessible as the Wallingford lot was. There were many other restaurants nearby. Finally, after twelve months of struggling, Dick went to the manager of a supplier to the Broadway store—Dohrman Hotel Supply—and said: "*We have enough money for our vendors. We have enough money for our payroll. We have enough money for our taxes. But we don't have enough money for you.*" He asked if they could defer payment to them for a month or two. To his relief, the manager said, "Request granted."

Broadway was tightly constrained by the limited parking. The store was also smaller. It was just not thriving. Dick and Ghorm were rapidly reaching the point when they were going to have to throw in the proverbial towel. Then, out of the blue, sales shot up overnight!

It turned out that Ivar's on Broadway—which was located one block north of *Dick's* just on the other side of the Broadway theater—closed to remodel their restaurant. Ivar's customers simply went to *Dick's* because it was so close. Dick was sure they would lose that business when Ivar's reopened, but they didn't. Their sales grew every month after that, and it is now one of *Dick's* busiest stores.

Dick's really had few competitors to speak of when they first opened in January 1954. There was only one other fast food hamburger place in Seattle that opened just two months before *Dick's* (named Gil's). And even though the corporate McDonald's started one year after *Dick's*, it was many years before McDonald's came to Seattle. By that time *Dick's* was well established. Today, *Dick's* is the oldest continuously operating "classic" fast food restaurant in Washington and Oregon.

After their experience at Broadway, the partners did not rush into a third store. *Dick's* on Holman Road did not open until 1960—five years later.

Holman Road cuts diagonally across northern Ballard into the Crown Hill neighborhood. Ghorm and Dick began looking for property there. This time, they found a piece of property that was in foreclosure, which gave them the chance to purchase their first property. They successfully negotiated an option on the land. While it never lost money like Broadway, it was slow to get started—but not so slow that it prevented them from opening another store three years later in Lake City.

Lake City opened in 1963, but its location made it a challenge. It was one block off the major thoroughfare—Lake City Way. When driving south on Lake City Way, people couldn't see it from the road, which posed a visibility and marketing problem.

Additionally, there were businesses across the street on 30th, but their front doors were on Lake City Way. Their messy back doors were across the street from *Dick's*—garbage and trash piled up there. It looked awful. Over the years, however, the businesses' owners realized that *Dick's* was good for their businesses, and they cleaned up the properties considerably. Despite these obstacles, Lake City did well from the beginning—it was the only other new restaurant with a fast start and was their largest property in terms of square feet until the Edmonds store opened many years later.

Dick's ventured briefly into Bellevue in 1965. The Bellevue Dick's was located on the northeast corner of Bellevue Way and 10th NE, across the street from the Bellevue Post Office. It was the only store to close. In 1973, *Dick's* was looking to open a store in Queen Anne. Realtor Henry Broderick was working with Coldwell Banker Realty at the time. Broderick, *Dick's,* and Carnation Dairy—one of *Dick's* main vendors all banked at SeaFirst Bank. Coldwell Banker was looking for property to build in Bellevue, and *Dick's* was looking for capital for the new Queen Anne store. Dick sold the land to Coldwell Banker in four days and was able to obtain a loan to build on Queen Anne.

Queen Anne opened in 1974. It is the only *Dick's* restaurant with indoor seating. Unfortunately, the partners found interior seating very expensive because it had to be heated, cleaned, and staffed. *Dick's* goal was to have the highest quality of food with the fastest service at the lowest prices. Because indoor seating added to costs, they decided no more stores with indoor seating.

No new *Dick's* restaurants opened between 1974 and 2011. Until 1991, the original partnership wanted to focus on operational excellence and the existing five restaurants. After Dick's partners sold their interests to Dick in 1991, Dick did not think they should add a new restaurant because of the debt the company took on to buy out the other partners, infrastructure costs, and potential span-of-control issues—it could turn out to be one too many restaurants to care for and manage effectively. After the buyout was finally paid off years later, his sons kept urging him to open another store, but Dick was reluctant. Finally, after Dick thought more about it, he concluded that while his sons were doing a great job, the one experience none of them had was opening a new restaurant. There were always problems when opening a new restaurant, he knew, and it took time to work them all out. Dick finally relented and consulted with them on what was needed to get a new store built.

Fawn Spady, Dick's daughter-in-law, had the idea of doing an online customer poll to select the new location because of the tremendous customer interest in the company's 40th and 50th anniversary *Memory Books*, which Fawn had proposed and previously managed.

The new location—Edmonds—was selected with the help of an online survey. The interest in the new site location was so keen that at one point, the high volume of ardent fans voting with online scripts slowed down the website of their voting contractor. All in all, 115,978 customers voted with about 45 percent voting to locate North, 27 percent for the South End, and 26 percent for the Eastside.

The Edmonds restaurant, on Highway 99, is presently the largest store in the system. Groundbreaking was May 19, 2011. Over 150 people attended, including the mayor and former mayor of Edmonds, the head of the Edmonds City Council, and the director of economic development for Snohomish county and the Snohomish County Executive, along with the winners of the groundbreaking contest, Dick's family, and several employees from the other stores and office. *Dick's* in Edmonds opened on October 20, 2011 with an estimated 800-1000 hungry fans attending the grand opening ceremony.

SOME STORE STORIES

Each store has a story. As mentioned, the first *Dick's* survived a blizzard in the first month after it opened. *Dick's* in Wallingford opened at a time when Catholics still ate fish on Friday. Friday nights were always crowded with students from the Catholic schools who would come at 11:45 p.m. to order hamburgers they could eat a minute after midnight—on Saturday.

Also mentioned earlier, Broadway almost didn't make it but began to thrive when Ivar's closed to remodel.

At the Holman store, Dick drew on his Seabee experience in World War II and dug the ditches and installed the sewer lines to the ditch running along Holman Road rather than pay someone else to do it.

Lake City had a fire, which closed the restaurant for 30 days. Dick had been at a meeting and stopped by the Lake City store. He saw the crew talking to each other very animatedly. He left and went home. He learned later that the grease to cook the French fries was getting too hot. The staff could not control the temperature. They did not think to cut off the electricity, and a fire broke out so fast and hot that the entire ceiling was black.

More recently, a customer leaving the Lake City store put the car in drive rather than reverse and slammed into the restaurant. Luckily, no customers were between the car and the restaurant.

Queen Anne, the only store with indoor seating, was also one of the first restaurants in Seattle to ban smoking. Once the study emerged linking secondhand smoke to cancer, *Dick's* banned smoking inside. "We put up 'No Smoking' signs all over the restaurant, but people kept tearing them down," Dick's son Jim observed. "There were a lot of upset customers who wanted to smoke with their meal. It took about a year, but things finally settled down."

The Queen Anne restaurant was also the location of an interview with Bill Gates, Jr. on the national TV program *60 Minutes*.

THE FOOD

Milkshakes

When *Dick's* started in 1954, new milkshake machines were just coming on the market at McDonald's in California. When Ghorm and Dick went there in 1953, most milkshakes were hand-dipped and individually whipped using high-speed multi-mixers. These took time to make, because when the milkshake mix was delivered, it was frozen solid and could not be dipped. When the vendor delivered the mix, the restaurant put it into a freezer storage unit to temper it 10 degrees for dipping. This made it possible to scoop the mix, weigh the mix, add milk and syrup, and then put the ready to whip milkshakes on multi-mixers.

As the original McDonald's grew into the corporate McDonald's, Ray Kroc, McDonald's corporate founder, substituted milkshake machines for hand-dipped shakes. This saved him building space because he no longer needed to temper the mix and he could produce shakes more rapidly. However, Dick and Ghorm felt this lowered the quality of the milkshakes, so *Dick's* did not use milkshake machines. Instead, they used their storage unit to temper the mix and continued to hand dip their shakes.

To create a *Dick's* milkshake, the milkshake mix is scooped out, and syrup and milk are added. As the shake spins, the content rises. When the mix is about an inch from the top of the container, the flavor and texture of the milkshake changes. Dick calls this the flavor blossom. This makes *Dick's* milkshakes such a superior product—because the milkshake is much smoother and the flavor more intense. Dick considers the milkshake to be their most unique product.

Dick's still makes only three flavors. Chocolate accounts for 50 percent of their milkshake sales; the other 50 percent is split pretty evenly between strawberry and vanilla.

When McDonald's arrived in Seattle a few years after *Dick's* opened, *Dick's* was well established and, fortunately, wasn't hurt by the competition. McDonald's busied itself with buying land, getting branded, and selling franchises at $30,000 to $40,000 per store—in addition to expensive advertising—something *Dick's* rarely did.

French Fries

French fries are temperamental too. *Dick's* uses the freshest potatoes grown locally in Washington and Idaho. *Dick's* has had long and excellent relations with their vendors, so they know the quality of the potatoes they serve. Dick said they had some "*pretty sorry spuds*" at the beginning. The color was not always right.

They treat their spuds as specially as they do their milkshake mix. When they arrive, the potatoes are put into a warm room, which helps to convert the sugar to starch. It improves their color and they stay crisp. *Dick's* does not skin the potatoes. Keeping the skin adds to the texture and flavor of the fries as well as making them more nutritious.

A recent challenge, however, was having to change the frying oils to eliminate trans fats as required by the county under its new public health regulations. *Dick's* now uses 100% High Oleic Sunflower oil.

QUALITY AND CONSISTENCY

It was Dick's and Ghorm's belief that quality and consistency were paramount to meet their customers' expectations and keep them happy. Consequently, there have been few changes at *Dick's* over the years. "*The Special*" with lettuce and *Dick's* secret sauce, and the *"Deluxe,"* a beefed-up quarter-pound special with cheese and *Dick's* secret sauce, were both added in 1971. Orange soda was dropped from the menu in the 1960's, and Diet Coke was added instead.

THE PARTNERS

By the 1970s, Ghorm was running the business, and the partners had finished their expansion. Dick had dealt largely with real estate, so he decided what he really wanted to do was go back to college and study for an MBA degree. He applied to and was accepted at the University of Washington.

Until 1991, Dick never really returned fulltime to *Dick's* after his work at the University of Washington. While he was in school, however, he did meet with each individual store manager on a one-on-one basis every three months for three years to help maintain the cohesiveness of the partnership. It was important to Ghorm and Dick that their employees knew they were interested in their work and that much was at stake in preserving a well-run business.

Dick's was originally formed as a partnership with three equal partners—Dick, Ghorm, and Dr. Thomas—although Ghorm and Dick were the only working partners. In 1991, Dick's children purchased Ghorm's and Thomas's shares and replaced the unlimited personal liability of the original general partnership with the limited personal liability of the new limited partners and also created a succession plan so that the management and ownership of *Dick's* would stay in the Spady family for generations to come.

GLOWING COMPANY CULTURE

What sets *Dick's* apart from other businesses— not just restaurant businesses—is how they treat their employees. *Dick's* is legendary in Seattle for its generosity. This is reflected in the Second Responsibility of a Successful Business, from their *Philosophy of Business Statement*:

> The Second Responsibility of a successful business is to treat its employees and

suppliers fairly—both are needed in order to deliver goods and services to **customers**, i.e., to the *public—the ultimate benefactors of a successful business.*

In this regard, *Dick's* provides the highest pay rate known in the industry in 2013 at $10.25 an hour to start and $10.75/hour after certain basic skills are learned, which normally takes 90 days. These are well above minimum wage. Employees working at least 24 hours per week also get 100% employer-paid medical insurance and are eligible to start a four-year, $22,000 college scholarship after just six months if they continue to work at least 20 hours per week. *Dick's* also pays its employees up to four hours extra pay per month for volunteering at any local charity, and it offers a 401(k) retirement plan with a 50% match (see Appendix 1).

Normal employee turnover in the fast-food industry, according to Jim Spady, Vice President, CEO and Corporate Legal Counsel for *Dick's*, is 100 to 200 percent a year. Many people in the industry are hired and quit in their first week. "It's a fast paced business. People are standing all day; they work hard and fast all day and move between hot and cold environments all the time. Many people just can't handle the pace," Jim says. At *Dick's,* there are two different shifts—10:30 a.m. to 6:30 p.m. and 6:30 p.m. to 2:30 a.m. They close only twice a year—for Thanksgiving and Christmas.

Since the 2008 downturn in the economy, Jim indicated, "our turnover has been its lowest ever—around 25 percent. Even the students who worked with us and chose a college degree are now staying on as other jobs are increasingly hard to find. The time when we had our highest turnover—bordering on 200 percent—was during the dot-com bubble in the late 1990s. But when that bubble burst, *Dick's* turnover returned to its typical 50 to 100 percent."

Staffing a fast food restaurant is a constant challenge, especially keeping a balance between new and experienced employees. "The first three months, a new employee is mostly in the way," Jim said. "Once they make it three months, they have learned the job; after six months, they are good at the job, and after a year, they can start conducting on-the-job training of the new hires. Apart from the few new hires to staff the Edmonds store, there were hardly any new employees in 2011 because so many people were staying on."

Opening the new store in Edmonds represented a staffing challenge. *Dick's* hired some new local people from Edmonds and started training them several weeks before the new store opened. But the new restaurant also needed lots of experienced employees as well and those had to come from the other stores. Fortunately, many of the experienced employees lived near Edmonds, so they could be transferred to the new store.

All *Dick's* stores are autonomous. The local store managers have the sole hiring and firing authority for their stores.

Dick's business philosophy and employee benefits have evolved over time. In the beginning they could not afford the benefits they offer now.

The scholarships, even though expensive, are another reason *Dick's* has a lower turnover. Because employees receive tuition support if they work three days per week, employees are more inclined to keep working at *Dick's,* thus reducing employee turnover. *Dick's* also gives credits for childcare as a substitute for tuition payment if the employee has children in day care but isn't going to college at the same time.

All in all, what the Spadys are most proud of is *Dick's* reputation: the fast, friendly service and low price. Everyone eats at *Dick's,* Jim notes — from the homeless to Bill Gates and Paul Allen.

"We are in the business of not changing. We want to be an island of stability in a sea of change—we have had few changes since 1954," Jim notes. "We want people to get the same good food they got the last time, every time. We have always used vegetable oil, never beef lard, to fry our potatoes but were challenged with the switch to the new non–trans fat oil, required by law. It was one of the few things we have changed over the years."

Dick's has received award after award for being an outstanding corporate citizen, including the 2000 Outstanding Philanthropic Small Business Award and the Seattle Municipal League's Business of the Year Award in May 2005, among numerous others.

All this is a long way from that first night of soggy onions on the floor in Wallingford and a tribute to the dream and goal of Ghorm and Dick who believed: *"To be successful in the restaurant business, the food must taste the same today as it did yesterday, last week, or last year."* It is a tradition *Dick's* has kept and honored.

Dick's Paternal Grandfather and Grandmother,
circa 1907, Portland, Oregon
Back row, from left: Henry, Grandfather John,
Grandmother Lena,
Front row, from left: Pauline, baby George on lap, and
John (Dick's father)

Dick with his mother Elsie, 1925

Dick in the U.S. Navy, 1943

Dick in the U.S. Air Force, 1952

Family at Seattle First United Methodist Church, June 1963
Back row, from left: Eula Arnold (Lou's mother), Dick, Bertie Lee Arnold (Lou's sister), Elsie Schmeer (Dick's mother). Middle row, left: Lou with baby Doug and Carol. Front row, from left: John, Jim, and Walt

Whole Family, 1991
Doug, Jim, Walt, Lou, Dick, Carol, John

Lou and Dick, 1999

Dick's 90th birthday celebration, 2013

Back row, from left:
Julie Spady, Tatyana Tsyrlina-Spady, Alex Spady with son Aiden, Danielle Spady, Chad Spady, David Donovan with wife Jasmine and Baby James, Saul Spady, Nan Avant-Spady, and Fawn Spady

Front row, from left:
Doug Spady, John Spady. Lou and Dick Spady, Greg and Peg Schmeer, Walt Spady, and Jim Spady

Edmonds Store Groundbreaking, May 2011
From left: Jim, Dick, Walt, Lou, and John

Jim and Dick at the Edmonds Groundbreaking, 2011

John and wife Tatyana Tsyrlina-Spady, 2010

John with his son Alex, grandson Aiden, and Santa, 2009

Jim with daughter Jasmine, son Saul, and
wife Fawn, 2011

Dick with second great grandchild Baby James, granddaughter Jasmine, son Jim, daughter-in-law Fawn, and grandson Saul, 2013

Dick and Walt, 2010

Walt and wife Nan Avant-Spady, 2012

Carol with her son Lucas James DesPres, 2005

Lucas James DesPres, 2011

From left: Ann Avant, Nan and Walt, Dick and Lou,
John and Tatyana, Danielle and Chad, Julie and Doug,
Jasmine and David Donovan, Fawn and Jim, 2010

Doug with daughter Danielle, son Chad, and wife Julie, 2013

**Doug, Dick, Walt, and Jim at the
Mount Si Golf Course, 2006**

**John and Dick with the Ravi Shankar Award for
Uplifting Human Values from The Art of Living
Foundation, February 2007**

Aiden Spady, Dick's first great grandchild, 2007

Chapter 4

PROPELLED BY VALUES, VISION AND VOICE

*W*hile thousands of customers know about *Dick's* Drive-In, most of those fans and customers know little about the man behind that name who has fought to ensure that the public can have its collective voice more easily heard in community decisions.

Armed with the social justice heritage of his church and its values, Dick took to heart the importance of being an engaged and active citizen. As a Protestant—a United Methodist—he knew the Church was neither infallible nor unmovable; the key relationship is between God and his people. As Dick says, "...we are taught in our theology that our responsibility is directly to God through Christ so there is no other person or institution between us (including the Church). That is very powerful theology because it means I am free… *to disagree and not be ostracized from the Church…. It is each individual member* who has that responsibility." This is the bedrock of Dick's values.

But Dick went one step further. "That all translates directly in the secular world to the equal responsibility of a citizen in the world."[1] Therein lies Dick's passion to give the public a voice. Our responsibility is not just to God, as Dick sees it; we have a responsibility to our community as well.

The Methodist Church grew out of the Anglican Church, known in America as the Episcopal Church. Historically, the Methodist Church has been very interested in social concerns. John Wesley, Methodist founder of the denomination, believed that "*the living core of the Christian faith is revealed in Scripture, illumined by tradition, vivified by experience, and confirmed by reason."* This is known as the Wesleyan Quadrilateral. This four-cornered philosophy is reflected in *Dick's* Philosophy of Business (see Appendix 1).

---

[1] *Leadership of Civilization Building,* pp. 35–36.

Methodists, therefore, he points out, do not believe in a literal interpretation of the Bible. Wesley had tried to get the Anglican Church to be more dynamic and engaging of its members. Lacking success in that effort, he founded the Methodist movement within the Anglican Church. It engaged its members by starting small dialogue or study groups of 12 members (the number of Apostles). These groups met to explore the Bible's teaching and to grow their faith. This approach led to the church's name, Methodist, because they had a "method" they followed to explore the Bible and its teachings, and to engage their members.

Later, Wesley trained and "ordained" two of his members to be superintendents with a laying on of hands and sent them to America to start the church there. Dick has always been influenced by both the *Social Principles* and the *Book of Resolutions of The United Methodist Church. They* played an important role in his life and led to his increasingly active service to others in community outreach.

In 1965 Dick was asked by the Rev. Joe Harding, the new Methodist superintendent, to become the Seattle District's Lay Leader and principal lay officer. The district then had 44 churches and about 25,000 members in the King County area. When he was asked to do this, Dick thought, *I think they have the wrong guy.*

The district lay leadership gave Dick a platform to find ways to engage church members—a path that would lead him to future efforts quite unrelated to *Dick's* Drive-In, but one that built on his passion for ensuring people have a voice in their organizations and institutions.

But, as Dick soon found out, discovering what people thought was hard work. He wanted to publish a survey in the district newsletter, but the church said they had no budget for that. He kept going to the different churches in the district to talk with their members about problems.

He also found out Robert's Rules of Order did not work well. People grabbed the microphone, got carried away, and roamed from topic to topic. The meetings weren't going well for either the members or the leadership.

The executive committee of the district board of laity had about 20 members and met monthly. They began experimenting with public engagement methodologies by having some forums among themselves. Their challenge was to find a way to give the public a voice. And it was a public that wanted to be heard. In all of his meetings at various churches, what their members consistently told Dick was: "We have no way to constructively contribute our opinions that are 1) *inherently beneficial* to us as individuals— through a process that itself has a payoff for our time and energy, 2) good for the church—which we love, and 3) good for the society as a whole of which we are a part. We are not an island by ourselves; we are part of something bigger."[2]

Also in 1965 his own local church in Bellevue actually split over an issue. Dick wondered if his church and its members could have been spared the pain of that break-up if there had been better feedback. *"How did it happen that good people of faith got to this point? Could the split have been prevented,"* Dick wondered, *"if there had been a way for people to anticipate problems earlier?"*

By the end of 1968 Dick's work as the district lay leader was at an end. Under the discipline of the time, he had to write an annual report. And he had to tell them the truth: *"The church would not succeed unless it gave the laity responsibility. The members were being paternalized to death,"* he said.

---

[2] *Leadership of Civilization Building,* p. 26

He thought his days as district lay leader were over. However, he would later be surprised to receive the Bishop's Medal in 2001 at the Pacific Northwest Annual Conference of the United Methodist Church.

Dick was finishing his work with the church in 1968—a turbulent year in America. The civil rights movement bloomed in the 1960s and was so eloquently framed by Martin Luther King Jr. in his 1963 "I Have a Dream" speech at the Lincoln Memorial. But his dream was tested in August of 1965 with the large-scale riot in the Watts neighborhood of Los Angeles. The riot lasted six days. By the time it subsided, 34 people had been killed, 1,032 injured, and 3,438 arrested. Then, in April of 1968, Martin Luther King Jr. was assassinated—a stunning stab at America's heart. His death touched off demonstrations across the country, as did the death of Robert Kennedy just two months later.

King's assassination drove Dick into action. He realized that since he was part of a larger society, he needed to do something to address the Watts riots and the King and Kennedy tragedies.

Dick thought the community should hold dialogues on race so people could prevent riots in their area and begin to hear each other's views and concerns on race. He started in Bellevue where he lived. He met with key leaders from the mayor and superintendent of public schools to the head of the chamber of commerce, the head of the Eastside YMCA, and other community organization leaders. They formed a new group—the *Eastside Inter-Racial Clearing House*—to hold low-key, informal face-to-face gatherings in people's homes or community settings. Over 400 people participated that first summer.

At the end of the summer, when the program was concluding, the *Eastside Inter-Racial Clearing House* steering committee decided to try one more thing—they would pair three black families with three white families. The groups would meet every Friday evening for three weeks to discuss constructive ways to address race relations in the community.

They used a new approach—they included all family members, not just the adults. Children who were too young to participate went to the YMCA gym to play together while the older children and adults were in their meetings. For many of these children, it was the first time they had actually played with children of a different race. Both John and Jim, Dick's two eldest sons, remarked that prior to that summer, they had never really been around anyone of color. Bellevue at the time was slowly growing and had few people of color. And because so many schools were de facto segregated, it was also the first time many of the children had any real interaction with others in racially mixed environments.

To discover what the program participants were thinking, Dick developed two products that would become pivotal in his future efforts: a special "*Opinionnaire*® Survey" and an analysis of its results that would be later known as a "*Fast Forum*® Report."

The interracial groups met on Fridays for three weeks in a row. Shortly before the end of the final meeting, Dick said, "We have been talking about the problems of race for over six hours now. It's time to take stock of where we are." He handed all those present a 3" x 5" index card and asked them to write what they thought the key problems were in race relations or offer some specific suggestion on how to improve them.

When the participants finished, they handed their cards to Dick, who numbered each card. Then, he passed the cards out again asking them to read the comments on the card thoughtfully. If they *clearly agreed with them*, they were to mark "yes"; if they *did not clearly agree*, they were to mark "no." If they did not want to answer the question at all, they should mark "abstain"—this last simple instruction would became a critical element later on to better understand a group's consensus rating. People placed their tally marks under three columns labeled "Yes," "No," and "Abstain."

After he passed out the cards, each person would respond, pass the card to the person on their left, and get a new card from the person on their right. The group completed the task in about 30 minutes. They left for the night, agreeing to meet one final time for a potluck dinner in one week.

Excitedly, Dick gathered his family, rushed home, put the kids to bed, and headed for the dining room table, pencil and paper in hand!

He quickly tabulated the responses by categories: youth/adult and black/white. He transferred the totals to the back of the cards and then reordered them by putting the largest total of "yesses" on the top. After reading them several times, Dick thought to himself, "*I think I understand how these people feel about race.*" Then the thought crept into his head, "*No, it's a stronger feeling than* *that—I believe I **know** how they feel about the problems of race."*

Dick did the same thing again with other groups over different weeks and tabulated their responses the same way. And the same thoughts kept creeping back. At the end, he was convinced he **knew** how the participants felt about race. But Dick was growing increasingly frustrated and was not sure how to give voice to it—he was aware something important was staring him in the face, and a growing awareness of a subtle but momentous idea kept nagging at him.

As Dick thought about these groups and the work he had done with the Methodist Church, he reflected that usually when a group of people get together, they immediately start by asking how they are going to proceed. If it is a large group, they usually choose *Robert's Rules of Order* as a guide. They then debate a particular approach, vote, and report out the majority opinion, but not the minority. The report usually just says that something had passed, but not that it passed by 51 percent or 95 percent. There is a big difference.

It dawned on Dick in reviewing the various group responses, that by allowing people to abstain, he could begin to see not only how people felt about an issue but also the degree of consensus on an issue. His approach meant one could still report out "yes," but could also now show how strongly people felt about that "yes."

So what did it mean if you had 228 who said yes, 153 who said no, and 207 who abstained? The numbers were so vast that it was hard to wrap your mind around it to discern the meaning. Dick solved that problem by framing it as an issue of polarization and consensus. In a vast oversimplification, if the above votes were on a specific issue, such as replacing the viaduct, for example, it would show that there was very little consensus on the issue. Nearly as many people said no as yes, and nearly as many again abstained. What this says to the astute politician is: "You have a problem on your hands; there is no clear consensus on this issue."

Most political or social polls typically allow only "yes" or "no" and "don't know/not sure." They don't offer the option to abstain. Dick thought that significantly limits the information leaders can access to make meaningful decisions. With most polls, there is no room for uncertainty or neutrality. Nor is there an opportunity to object to the question being asked. Most polls also don't identify degrees of consensus or disagreement.

What Dick was able to do over the years while refining his techniques was to provide a survey tool that charted polarization and consensus. His first survey tool used a scale of three—"yes," "no," and "abstain." Over the years, it became a five-part survey response with three being neutral, and answers ranging from strongly agree and agree, to disagree and strongly disagree. By including "abstain", and later on the option to "object" to the wording of a question, additional insights into an issue could be realized.

Being able to identify a degree of consensus helps decision makers chart a course of action because they can assess if agreement or disagreement is strong or weak—which can impact the course of an action and the likelihood of its success. So, if the spread of responses were better understood, an astute politician would likely probe further and listen more closely, or start another public education campaign to better communicate with the public.

Dick's experiences as district lay leader and with the *Eastside Inter-Racial Clearing House* forums led him to the decision to take a leave from *Dick's* to pursue a Master's degree in Business, so that he could build a better business for *Dick's.* This was when a professor said a word that would change the course of Dick's life forever.

Chapter 5

A WORD THAT CHANGED A LIFE AND FOSTERED A NEW BODY OF RESEARCH

*I*n 1968, Dick enrolled in the Graduate School of Business Administration at the University of Washington with a concentration in administrative theory and organizational behavior. His intent was to complete a Master's degree, and possibly a PhD, and develop a personal philosophy of business and leadership with the intent of returning to *Dick's* later on. But one word, spoken in class by his professor, would completely change his plans.

After he was admitted, he went to see the dean— Borge Saxberg—and told him of his experience with the church and his interest in developing some feedback mechanisms. He asked for permission to select Cecil H. Bell, a new faculty member whose recent PhD was in social psychology, to be his advisor.

Dick enrolled in Bell's first class. In the first two weeks, Dick had a flash of insight—what happened with his church was not simply a church problem; it was an organizational problem! The inability to communicate was not just an issue for the Methodists in this northwest corner of the country; it was a universal problem. That realization embedded itself in his head and drove him on more assuredly.

Soon afterwards Bell used the word "*Zeitgeist*," which Webster's Dictionary defines as "*the general moral, cultural, and intellectual spirit of an era*." Bell, reaching for the right word himself, said: "In the course of an organization's development, a kind of... of... Zeitgeist emerges." That was the first and last time Dr. Bell ever used that term in class. But it stuck with Dick—and completely rearranged his intellectual landscape.

He was hooked on *Zeitgeist* and its implications— but those implications, as he would discover, would lead him beyond business as usual.

Dick was rolling the word around in his mind, digesting the measure of its implications, when he had a new class assignment from a different professor. Dr. Theodore "Ted" Barnowe taught an advanced class in management theory. One day he gave his class a term paper assignment: "Just take anything in management theory and make it sound rational." Dick locked onto the assignment.

He began his project and wrote down everything he could think of *"that tended to move all organizations universally toward solving their problems and/or anticipating or adapting to changes in their internal or external environments."*

This assignment focused Dick's thinking and led to the formulation of his original eight theories of organization and management that he would later expand to 10. Dick thought, *"If these dynamics are true, then to function properly, any human organization or institution* must *have an effective feedback communication system."*

Dick called that feedback mechanism *Zeitgeist Communication* — a process that would communicate ideas not just one way: top to bottom or "one to many," it would also spread the idea *across and upward or* "many to many" in an organization or society. Most organizations and institutions today have no such structured mechanism for feedback communication.

Dick recognized most communication was from one source to many people via media, books, lectures, and speeches. There was no functional way for people to give meaningful feedback to leaders—public or private.

Dick thought most public opinion polls were flawed as well. They simply gave a picture of how people felt on an issue—yea or nay—just a snapshot in time. But those polls could not tell the degree of consensus on an issue. Dick wanted something that would produce a better road map and let leaders know if they were standing on solid ground or thin ice.

A feedback loop, however, had to be timely, streamlined, and structured. The feedback wouldn't work at all if it had to be tabulated by hand. One of the things Dick quickly realized in tabulating all the responses on those 3" x 5" index cards from previous discussions on race was that tabulating X's by hand was a mind-numbing exercise. To make the analysis he wanted, it would have to be done more quickly and accurately, and that meant learning to use a computer—something he had never experienced at OSU back in 1950. His curiosity led him to the Academic Computer Center at the University of Washington.

This was 1968. Computers as we know them today did not exist. Instead, they were giant "mainframes" filling entire rooms. Programs and data existed as small holes punched onto stiff paper cards, which were then read by a mechanical card reader and submitted to the computer in the back room. Dick's life journey now added a new path of information technology to his other paths of restaurants and administrative theory and communications.

His eldest son, John, recalls, "When I was around 11, my father brought home an interesting piece of 'new technology' for the times—an IBM 029 keypunch machine. He had started learning how to use it while taking classes at the university, but all his time away from the family convinced him to rent a machine and use it at home. We all appreciated having dad around more often. I learned to type and program computers too— just so I could help out and we could be together more often. He exemplified my own future civic collaborations with organizations like the National Coalition for Dialogue and Deliberation (www.ncdd.org)."

Dick was trying to create a computer program that would help him tabulate his data. He knew where he wanted to go but not how to get there. The computer programmers, he hoped, would give him the tools he needed. And they did.

Dick's information technology journey covers computer languages starting with COBOL on a University of Washington mainframe (written for Dick by programmer John Jacobsen). Dick and his son John then used Pascal and also HyperCard on the Apple Macintosh. Finally, the Fast Forum® computer program was rewritten as a web application—independent of platforms—and allowed one version to be maintained for all users.

So, armed with the theory, the practical tools, and his innate vision and entrepreneurship, Dick wanted to explore the interconnection of administrative theory and *Zeitgeist Communications.* He founded the nonprofit Forum Foundation in 1970 to do just that. He again had a social platform. His two co-founders of the Forum Foundation were Dr. Cecil Bell, the professor who had introduced him to Zeitgeist, and the Rev. William Ellington, PhD (theology)—both graduates from Boston University. Ellington at the time was a director of evangelism of The United Methodist Church in Nashville.

Dick defined the Administrative Process as: *"DIAGNOSE the problem; THEORIZE its solution;*

DECIDE what to do about it; ACCOMPLISH what was decided; and REVIEW what was done. It is an on-going process."

Dick realized, however, that the administrative process leads to an internal paradox: if feedback indicates things are okay, you simply stop looking. But if you fail, you keep looking for reasons why. *"Therefore, I have learned more from my mistakes than my successes,"* he observed.

With the Forum Foundation established, Dick continued his research. This time, his work was with the Church Council of Greater Seattle, which represented 17 different judicatories (synagogues and temples) and over 300 local churches. His portfolio for the council was "Futures Research." But the council was not interested in forecasting the future; it was interested in *foretelling* the future by having members of the various congregations identify what was important to them for the future of their faith communities. His research led to Dick's active participation in the World Future Society, an international nonprofit scientific consortium of people who study how social, economic, and technological developments are shaping our future.

In the early 1980s, Dick met the Rev. Kenneth B. Bedell, PhD, who had written the first book on computers and their role and use in the Methodist Church. The following year both men co-founded the Church Computer Users Network (CCUN) as a grassroots learning group. Bedell was elected president and Dick vice president. They also helped form the Circuit Writers Network, (so named after rural ministers who were "circuit riders" serving communities too small to have a full-time minister) and Ecunet, an organization that survives to this day.

Dick's hungry mind led him to become active in yet another group: the Religious Futurists Network, an outgrowth of the First Global Conference on the Future of the World Future Society held in Toronto, Canada, in 1980. Dick attended that conference as the official representative of the Church Council of Greater Seattle. He later met the Rev. Richard S. Kirby, PhD, from London, at the 1993 World Future Society conference in Washington, D.C. Dr. Kirby was elected international chair of the World Network of Religious Futurists in 1993. Dick would later ask Dr. Kirby to lead the new Stuart C. Dodd Institute for Social Innovation that Dick established in 1997.

For 14 years, Stuart Dodd headed the Washington State Public Opinion Laboratory at the University of Washington and was the leading authority on typical polling in the Northwest. Dick described Dodd as being *"a genius and yet as common as an old shoe."*

Dick still vividly recalls the first time he met Dodd in his office and outlined his administrative theories and communications research. *"As I was leaving with my hand on the doorknob, Dodd said, 'Dick, don't ever let anyone tell you that what you are doing is not important.' "* Dick and Dodd met at the Evergreen Chapter of the World Future Society in Seattle. Dodd had been brought to the University of Washington as a Walker-Ames Scholar and ended up staying 30 years. He served on the board of the Forum Foundation from 1973 until his death in 1975.

The Evergreen Chapter of the World Future Network sent a letter to Governor Dan Evans in 1973 urging him to do a futures study in Washington State patterned after the 1970 *"Hawaii 2000"* project. The *"Alternatives for Washington"* program ran from 1974–1977, and it remains a classic example of citizen participation from that time.

There are three words that are not included in Dick's prodigious vocabulary: *can't*, *won't*, and *quit*. Or as Dick says, *"I learned long ago that if something needs to be done, one has to get organized to do it."* He organized the Stuart C. Dodd Institute to encourage scholarly research on Dodd's work. Dodd's work on a mathematical cosmology is *"not for the faint of heart,"* as Dick says. So, he invited his colleague, Dr. Richard S. Kirby, to head the institute to continue Dodd's research. Kirby had just finished his PhD in theology at King's College in London in 1992. Dick offered him a home and an office owned by *Dick's* for public service activities. Kirby came to Seattle in 1995 and became Executive Director of the Stuart C. Dodd Institute for Social Innovation in 1997. He served in this capacity until his death in 2009.

As much as Dick loves research and believes theory is an essential foundation, he also believes theories should not just sit on shelves. They should be preludes to action—as Washington State and local elected officials would come to learn.

One of the central motivations in Dick's research is leadership. But what, he wondered, is leadership? *"It's obviously not something one does by oneself. And if there is leadership, it requires moving others to action, which requires communication. But if it involves communication, is it just one way—from leader to follower?"* That couldn't be true, he speculated, because you would end up like his church—with members feeling they were being "paternalized" to death. *"Was leadership a poll to test which way the wind was blowing? No. A poll was only a snapshot in time. That was not leadership. It only measured the depth of a river in one particular spot—it couldn't tell you if there were rapids, a waterfall, or smooth sailing ahead.*

"Leaders," he concluded, *"must be actively engaged with others."* This insight led Dick to his idea of "Many-to-Many Communication," so leaders would have a feedback loop and the people working with them would have a way for their voices to be heard and to become leaders as well.

Leadership doesn't exist in a vacuum. It thrives on working with and listening to others. It thrives on figuring out "who I am and where I am going." But leadership also depends on others to work out *how* we are going to get there. Leadership, therefore, is the art of human collaboration; the art of *civilization building.* "So it all began— *social innovation and civilization building*—the organizational and societal quest of people working together to improve their own future and that of the human race," Dick said.

Dick has spent the years since 1965 giving voice to that vision and giving voice to others.

Interestingly enough, Dick believes that the Achilles' heel of democracy is the large meeting:

> *Big meetings at often remote distances are the Achilles' heel of the democratic process which undergirds our society, public and private. ... Most big meetings intended for participation of members are a problem. People don't have the time and energy to go to big meetings—especially at remote distances. The logistics at such meetings are such that only a few people get to talk and most people can only listen. Emotions often run high and people and leaders frequently become exhausted from the cumbersome efforts to communicate to create consensus.*[3]

Or, as Dr. Jacob Bronowski wrote in his award-winning book, *The Ascent of Man*:

> *Science is the art of what is. Ethics is the world of what ought to be...[There are those who are] in love with the aristocracy of the intellect. And that is a belief that can*

---

[3] *The Search for Enlightened Leadership, Vol. 2, p. 21.*

only destroy civilization that we know. If we are anything, we must be a democracy of the intellect. **We must not perish by the distance between people and government, and between people and power."** [4]

This is Dick's life beyond *Dick's* Drive-in. The theoretical foundations of his research and theories can be found in his major work, which he co-authored with Richard Kirby and collaborated on with Cecil Bell: *The Leadership of Civilization Building: Administrative and Civilization Theory, Symbolic Dialogue, and Citizen Skills for the 21*[st] *Century*. ISBN: 0-9700534-9-5.

He has taken this theoretical foundation and given voice to others in King County and around the world—earning him an honorary doctorate from The Russian Academy of Education along the way.

---

[4] *The Ascent of Man (1973), 435, and TV series, emphasis added.*

Chapter 6

A VOICE FOR THE VISION

*I*f there are three words that are not in Dick's vocabulary, there are another three words that Dick Spady takes *very* seriously: "*We the People.*" He firmly believes our elected officials rule by our election of them—they derive their authority *from us* and serve at *our pleasure*, not theirs.

People have struggled for decades to have their voices heard. The problem of being heard has only increased today with the explosion of e-mail messages, TV and radio channels, blogs, tweets, and texting. In the late 1980s advertising agencies would tell their clients that a person would have to "hear" a message four times by the time they realized they had heard it the "first time." There seems even less hope of being heard now as an individual, because we have moved from three major national TV stations to well over 1,000 plus cable channels and from two daily newspapers in Seattle down to one. There has also been an explosion of hundreds of Seattle blogs, but with seemingly few opportunities for organized feedback from the general public.

The people's "voice" is often reduced to polls that are conducted at anyone's whim on numerous topics—usually crafted by polling companies that did not ask the public what was important to them.

Dick's research, however, has shown if you change the nature of the poll, you can find new information to make wiser and more informed decisions.

Dick's insights into *Zeitgeist Communications* led to his creation of a special *Opinionnaire®* Survey tool and its accompanying *Fast Forum®* Report. Together they provided a way for "many-to-many" people to communicate and more broadly understand one another's opinions. It also provided a format to send that knowledge back up to leadership so they could better understand participants' thoughts on a particular issue.

The *Fast Forum®* Report provides the means to communicate back to public or private leaders. Unlike typical polls, however, *Fast Forum®* Reports enable everyone who participates to learn quickly and succinctly where there are areas of consensus and common ground and where there are not. People can abstain from answering a question and even object if they think a question is inappropriate or misleading. It also allows people to respond privately and anonymously rather than having to stand up in public to voice their opinion.

We have all seen examples of a question that was improperly worded: "Have you stopped beating your dog?" comes to mind. Either yes or no yields the same answer—you beat your dog at some point in time, if not now. The *Opinionnaire®* Survey allows people to object to that kind of poorly worded question, rather than just having the choice of simply replying yes or no.

Here is an example of what happens when "abstain" and "object" are added to a survey. Let's take health care as an example: What would happen if you had answers ranging from 35% favoring government run health care and 35% thought it should be a personal responsibility, like automobile insurance. But 15% objected to the wording and another 15% abstained—they were just plain unsure or did not hold strong opinions one way or another.

As a public policy official, these numbers would tell you that proposing a specific health care solution would be political suicide. There is no consensus and considerable disagreement. These numbers show that a policy leader would have to conduct a major educational campaign to better inform the minds of the people who objected or abstained. But what if the number of objectors were larger, such as another 30%? That would indicate that people felt the question wording was totally misleading or inappropriate. This should lead you to think about other questions or language that could be used instead.

In other words, the ability to 'abstain' and 'object' offers a way of providing feedback to elected officials, or industry, or religious and community leaders of the *'Zeitgeist'* of their constituents in ways that were not possible before. It also helps to chart potential courses of action and insights for leaders to consider further.

One would think politicians would leap at this. The opposite seems to be true.

The Rev. William Cate, former President-Director of the Church Council of Greater Seattle, used Dick's methodology with considerable success: "I used the *Opinionnaire®* Survey approach for my own sake while I was at the Church Council of Seattle. I wanted to find out where the Church Council was on some key issues and we used the *Fast Forum®* Reports to great advantage. I knew where the Churches were on any given issue. It was great information that I would not have had otherwise."

THE CITIZEN COUNCILOR NETWORK

The *Fast Forum®* Reports and the *Opinionnaire®* Survey are at the heart of Dick's dream of "civilization building," civic engagement, and citizen councilors. The *Opinionnaire®* came from Dick's early survey work with churches, the *Eastside Inter-Racial Clearing House*, his research at the University of Washington, and the Forum Foundation through rapid advances in the information technologies of the time.

Filled with the conviction that the people's voice must be heard Dick went to the Washington State legislature in 1980 to lobby for a bill that would establish a Citizen Councilor Network where state voters could meet in small groups (eight to 12 people), review materials on an issue, have a conversation about it, and provide their opinions back by answering an *Opinionnaire*® Survey. These responses in turn would be directed to Citizen Councilor Coordinators and Deputy Coordinators, housed in the State Auditor's office. The State Auditor would prepare reports and send them to the participants, the legislature, the governor, and the media.

Dick never succeeded with a Citizen Councilor Network law at the state level. But in 1993 Dick received recognition for his efforts from Senate Resolution 1993-8636 honoring "...*the Forum Foundation for its excellent work and research to improve communication in organizations and society... and to encourage the further innovative research of the Forum Foundation in its civilization education programs for communities and educational programs in schools.*"

Never one to quit when he believed in something, Dick turned next to Martin Luther King Junior County.

In 2007, at the age of 83, Dick focused on King County and introduced the *Easy Citizen Involvement Initiative,* Initiative 24, which required the collection of voter signatures. By the time the initiative was filed, Dick had only 90 days to collect 55,000 signatures—the number of signatures needed to qualify the initiative for legislative action.[5] The Spady family pulled together and ended up collecting over 80,000 signatures with two weeks to spare! A signature gatherer said people loved the initiative and told Dick that it was an honor to collect voters' signatures for this initiative.

Because of the popular response to the initiative, Dick was able to get a hearing with the King County Council. The council had two choices: it could pass the initiative into law or let it automatically go on the ballot in the next election. The council could not simply ignore the measure. For the first time ever with this type of initiative, the King County Council decided to enact the initiative directly by ordinance and voted unanimously to create the Citizen Councilor Network. The program it subsequently created was called the *Countywide Community Forums* of King county.

The Preamble of the ordinance adopted by King County states:

---

[5] *The required numbers are derived from a formula based on the percentage of people who voted in the previous election of the King County Executive.*

One key to a sustainable community is an informed and sustainable dialogue among leaders and people. Citizens need new, more convenient, and effective ways to share their opinions with other citizens and the leaders of their organizations, institutions, and governments. This is a process of <u>building social capital</u> through both bonding and bridging dialogue and improving community mental health and happiness...

Recognizing that large public meetings can be difficult forums to capture accurate portraits of public opinion—they go on too long, are often dominated by the loudest voices, and do not offer a constructive way to find common ground— Dick focused initially on small, in-person group discussions but a year later added an online survey option.

Any civic-minded participant or organization can host a face to face forum. Participants are told that the purpose of their meeting is not to find fault, cast blame, or criticize, but rather to find areas of common ground, or not, and report back to the county on what they all think about the issue being considered.

Over 4,500 people participated in the countywide forums since 2007. Nine topics were completed by the time the privately funded program ended in 2011 (reference the King County Auditor's Office at www.tinyurl.com/ccf-reports):

1. *Transportation (3/08);*
2. *Public Policy and Choices (7/08);*
3. *Values and Performance of King County Government (6/09);*
4. *Public Safety, Law, and Justice (10/09);*
5. *Improving Customer Service and Public Engagement in King County (6/10);*
6. *Citizen Priorities for Government during Challenging Economic Times (10/10);*
7. a) *Equity and Economic Opportunity (5/11);*
   b) *New Framework for Public Engagement in Unincorporated King County (8/11);*
8. *King County Budget: Achieving Sustainability Together (9/19).*

Working with diverse groups and using the *Opinionnaire®* Survey to identify the range of responses on a given issue helped to ensure that a broad range of voices were heard. The ongoing challenge for the Countywide Community Forums was sustainable funding, apart from the personal funding from Dick himself. Another challenge was finding the best way to "frame" an issue so the public better understands the context in which the questions were asked.

In 2010, Dick was named Citizen Councilor Coordinator *Emeritus* in recognition of his work in sponsoring this initiative. Meaningful civic engagement is an ongoing challenge and another is convincing participants that they can have a voice and that their own vision and voices will actually be heard.

A statewide version of the Community Forums model operated from 2012-2013 (on Twitter @CFNetwork); a national version of the model (on Twitter @NatDialogue) received a Catalyst Award grant in 2012 from the National Coalition for Dialogue and Deliberation (www.ncdd.org/10940); and a student-led model focused on the issue of immigration remains active (on Twitter @AIForums).

INTERNATIONAL HONORS: THE BROAD REACH OF IDEAS

Dick first became interested in Russia when the Goodwill Games were held in Seattle in 1990. Thousands of Russians came for the games and needed places to stay. Dick's Bellevue Overlake Rotary Club hosted several visitors and his guest was Marat Akylbekov from the city of Bishkek in what is now Kyrgyzstan (formerly Kirghizia in the USSR). At the time, Marat was a Komsomol member, which was considered a Soviet youth organization.

While neither could speak the other's language, Dick and Marat managed to communicate about many things, and Marat took a copy of Dick's manuscript, *The Leadership of Civilization Building*, when he returned home. He also invited Dick and Lou to visit him in Bishkek. Dick hoped that Marat would find a good translator and scholars there who might be interested in his leadership theories.

Marat gave Dick's manuscript to Almas Chukin, an assistant professor of economics at a state university in Bishkek. When Chukin read Dick's frontispiece on the characteristics of good leaders and poor leaders, he said, "The left-hand side is what we know of leadership in the Soviet Union. What we need to do now is learn the characteristics of the good leaders in the right-hand column."

The following is the chart from *The Leadership of Civilization Building* that Chukin referenced:[6]

---

[6]   Frontispiece, *The Search for Enlightened Leadership,* Volume One, Pan Press, 1996

Administrative Theories and Realities

Superficial Administrative Ideas Held by Most Leaders	Administrative Reality
1. The management process is: Plan, Organize, Motivate, and Control.	1. The administrative process is: Diagnose, Theorize, Decide, Accomplish, and Review.
2. I have the authority here to govern other individuals.	2. Other individuals here must give me my authority to govern them.
3. I'm in charge; I have the power.	3. My power is derived from the consent of others.
4. I can fire anybody, anytime.	4. Anybody can leave me, anytime.
5. My job is to get the job done.	5. My job is to help others get the job done.
6. What we need is knowledge.	6. What we need is wisdom.
7. I have to lead everyone— I am the leader.	7. Everyone is a leader.
8. I am superior to others.	8. Others are equal to me.
9. The basic organizing principle of the human race is A over B over C over D etc. [A>B>C>D . . .] which is an Authoritarian Hierarchy (Authoritarianism and Totalitarianism); it provides no checks or balances in governance with minimum societal incentives.	9. The basic organizing principle of the human race is A (Administrators) over B (Bureaucrats) over C (Citizens) over A (Administrators) [A>B>C>A . . .] which is a Participative Heterarchy (Freedom and Democracy); it provides checks and balances in governance with maximum societal incentives.
10. "Governors" (leaders) have responsibility and authority—ultimately.	10. "People" (constituents) have responsibility and authority—ultimately.

Almas then invited Dick to come and lecture. Dick and his wife, Lou, were poised to visit in 1991, when then Russian Premier Mikhail Gorbachev was ousted in a coup. But as soon as Gorbachev was reinstated a few days later, Dick and Lou were on a plane bound for Moscow. It was the very year that would witness the end of the Union of Soviet Socialist Republics in December.

Almas and Marat flew to Moscow to meet Dick and Lou and showed them all around the city. Then, the four flew to Kyrgyzstan, accepting Marat's invitation to reciprocate Dick and Lou's generosity. When they arrived, Almas was no longer teaching. He had been appointed instead to head the Department of Industry at the Kyrgyz Ministry of Economics and Finance. Lou and Dick were hosted by the government for one week and then took the Trans-Siberian Railway back to Moscow and St. Petersburg, passing within 50 miles of Dick's paternal grandfather's birthplace in Norka, Russia, near present-day Saratov.

These connections were to become even deeper. In 1992, Dick and his son Jim attended a conference of the Association for Moral Education in Athens, Georgia, where Dick was giving a presentation on his research. As an international association, it attracted educators from all over the world. Jim was very concerned about the quality of education in America, so he joined his father at the conference.

Professor Tatyana Tsyrlina, a prominent Russian educator in the Department of Education at Kursk State University, in Kursk (a city about 350 miles southwest of Moscow), also participated and presented at the conference and happened to attend Dick's presentation. Tatyana later met John, Dick's eldest son, and the two were married in 2007.

In 1995, while attending another conference on moral education in England, Tatyana met Arthur Ellis, PhD, professor and director of the Center for Global Curriculum Studies at Seattle Pacific University. She asked Art if he knew Dick Spady. Art said no but when asked whether he knew *Dick's* Drive-In, he immediately said yes. A week later, Dick showed up in Art's office, and they began a long professional relationship.

Tatyana's interest in Dick's leadership and civic engagement work led her to translate all three volumes of Dick's leadership series into Russian:

- *The Search For Enlightened Leadership, Volume I: Applying New Administrative Theory,* and

Volume II: Many-To-Many Communications

and his major work:

- *The Leadership of Civilization Building: Administrative and Civilization Theory, Symbolic Dialogue, and Citizen Skills for the 21st Century.*

In 1998, Dick returned again for a sixth and final trip to Russia to attend another educational conference. When the president of Dick's Bellevue Overlake Rotary Club learned he was going to Russia, he informed the Rotary International district governor of District 5030. The governor asked Dick to take the first steps to start a Rotary Club in Kursk, Russia. When Dick arrived in Kursk, Tatyana's hometown, he asked her to bring some people together to see if they were interested in starting a Rotary Club. It happened that Tatyana herself and a few of her friends also wanted to become involved in Rotary activities. She arranged for a dinner with them and invited Dick to come and discuss Rotary. Dick served as the scribe.

This was no ordinary dinner—it consisted of many different courses. Dick was full by the time he had finished the fourth one. When the waiters came through the door with a fifth course, he threw his hand up saying he simply could not eat any more!

A year and a half later, their seed group had attracted enough other people to formally register, and they had their first official Rotary meeting. The district governor for this (then) European district came from *Sweden* to charter the club. The second president of the Kursk Rotary Club was Tatyana, thus placing her among the first female Rotary presidents in Russia.

Russian interest in Dick's work was high and remains so. In the course of his travels to and from Russia, he was introduced to academics Boris Bim-Bad and Nikolay Nikandrov. Bim-Bad was president of the University of the Russian Academy of Education, and Nikandrov was president of the Russian Academy of Education. In 2003, the Russian Academy of Education awarded Dick the title of *Honorary Doctor of Humanities, D.Litt,* for "contributions to Russian Democracy and Higher Education."

Dick wore a cap and gown, and the degree was presented by Dr. Arthur Ellis on behalf of the Russian Academy of Education during a ceremony at the University Temple Methodist Church in Seattle.

The degree was signed by Professor Bim-Bad. This recognized a lifetime of research and action on the important task of leadership development, civic engagement, and democracy.

Dick's wife and family have been mentioned only briefly until now. But the rock that held him through his works all these years and gave him a home and a family was a southern belle named Ina Lou Arnold, who arrived in Seattle in 1954 as an ensign in a naval uniform and who spoke with a lilting southern drawl. Dick was defenseless. They were married on August 5, 1955.

Chapter 7

FAMILY LIFE

*N*o story of Dick's life would be complete without sharing his interests and his love for his wife and family. Lou and Dick have five children: John (1956), Jim (1957), Walt (1959), Carol (1960), and Doug (1963).

Being raised in Portland, Oregon, on the shores of the Columbia River and in the shadow of Mount Hood, Dick developed a love for and enjoyment of the outdoors. As a young man, he skied downhill from Timberline Lodge on Mount Hood and followed increasingly complex cross-country trails down to Government Camp near the base of the mountain.

While he worked most of his childhood as well as going to school, Dick still found time to be involved in sports—gymnastics and softball.

Barely breaking 149 pounds well into his adulthood, Dick was the size and shape to excel in gymnastics. His favorite routines were on the horizontal bar and the rings. He used his lunch hour to work out and could perform "around the world" on the horizontal bar. One day, when he was working on an academic project with one of his high school teachers, the teacher looked at his hands and asked, "How did you get calluses like that?" Dick told him about the horizontal bar and the rings.

His interest in gymnastics continued into college. One day, his Oregon State University (OSU) coach received a call from the gym coach at Albany High School, who invited him to come to Albany with a couple of the gymnasts, Dick was selected as one of them. Each gymnast was asked to give a demonstration of his skills. Dick was the only one to perform an "around the world." Though he never had any training by a coach on how to do this, he excelled with a lot of practice, learned by watching, and taught himself by trial and error.

Dick was also active in the fraternal DeMolay International, the young men's division of the

Freemasons. In what would be a lifelong pattern of Dick's endeavors, he excelled in his work and became a master counselor with the responsibilities of a president.

While at OSU, Dick joined the Alpha Delta chapter of the Theta Xi fraternity. He became the chapter president for a year when he was a junior. While he was president, his chapter participated in a national competition of excellence, which was based on members' grade point averages (GPA) and excellence in intramural sports and campus activities. His chapter won the National Memorial Competition in 1951 based on the chapter's performance in 1950, when he was president.

With college and a year's tour of duty in Korea behind him and his dream of starting his own business being realized, Dick turned his attention to starting a family of his own. After moving to Seattle, he became active in his church and joined its group for single young adults. In 1954, the same year they opened the first *Dick's*, he went to a late-summer Methodist youth retreat at Seabeck on Hood Canal, where he met Ina Lou Arnold from Georgia. It was kismet.

Lou, as she preferred to be called, had been watching him play volleyball. New to Seattle, she had recently been taken to the new *Dick's* on Wallingford by a folk-dancing partner who wanted to treat her to "the best milkshake in the city." She'd just had that milkshake a week before she went to the Seabeck retreat, so it was still fresh in her mind when she met Dick. And, as Dick relates, the combination of her navy uniform and her Southern lilt made her irresistible to him. They were married on August 5, 1955, in the chapel of the Seattle First United Methodist Church, which was then on 5th and Columbia downtown. Within a year and a half Dick had managed to realize two of his dreams—starting a business and starting a family.

Lou was born and raised in Rossville, Georgia— way up in the very northwest tip of Georgia, *"just six blocks from Tennessee,"* as she says. Her elementary school was in Georgia, but her high school was in Chattanooga, Tennessee. After high school, she attended the University of Chattanooga (now University of Tennessee at Chattanooga), where she received her bachelor's degree in economics and commerce in 1953.

After graduation Lou worked at the Tennessee Valley Authority (TVA) as an assistant to the plant manager, *not* as a secretary. She remembers measuring all the dirt the crews moved when they were building dams.

Wanting to spread her wings and venture to new and different places, Lou decided to "join the navy and see the world." She enlisted in Nashville but had to fly to Macon, Georgia, to be sworn in during March of 1954.

After her commission, she spent three months training in Newport, Rhode Island, and was then assigned to Seattle to be a cryptographic officer, arriving four months later on July 1. As a cryptographer, she had a security clearance and worked in a small room with six other cryptographers, who used machines to follow secret dispatches after the Korean War.

Lou immediately fell in love with Seattle. Having been raised in the hot, humid South, she loved Seattle's cool summer evenings. *"You could wear a sweater in July. I loved it."*

Dick and Lou made their first home on a small houseboat at the southeast end of Lake Union near what is now ZymoGenetics and the Lake Union Dry Dock. Lou became pregnant right away, so they looked for a new place where they would not have to worry about their soon-to-be-eldest son, John, crawling off the deck into the lake.

Dick and Lou found a house on the south end of Capitol Hill just down the street from St. Joseph Catholic Church on 18th Avenue E. They purchased the home from an estate for $10,500, but it needed a lot of work. Even with help from "Dad" Swanson, a retired contractor who lived next door to the restaurant in Wallingford, it still took them three weeks to fix it up, paint it, clean it, and move in. They would live there from 1956 to 1962 as more children after John were born. Soon with three boys and a girl, the family needed more space and decided to move to Lake Sammamish in Bellevue.

In 1959, Lou and Dick bought some land on the lake, but it was an oddly shaped lot. It had a large area at the front of the property, with a narrower leg that went down to the lake. They hired an architect, but it took them three years to get the right design and build on the site. They finally moved there in 1962. Unlike their home on Capitol Hill, it had *lots* of bedrooms and bathrooms to accommodate a future houseful of teenagers. They had many neighbors who also had kids, and there were plenty of woods and a lake to play in.

Dick loved being on the lake. There were so many things for the children to do—woods to explore and the lake for swimming, fishing, or boating. When the kids turned 16, as Dick said, *"I gave them a small motorboat instead of keys to a car."*

Looking back on living there, Dick's second son, Jim, remembers it being an idyllic childhood—only the west side of the lake was largely developed at the time so there was plenty of fishing, swimming, and waterskiing.

One day, a stray dog they eventually called Spot showed up. He was smart and had a good personality, so they kept him—outside at first, then in and out later. It wasn't until after Spot died that they discovered he had been making rounds every day to all the neighbors and getting treats on the side.

Lake Sammamish was not just any lake. It had a resident seal named Butch (see www.HistoryLink.org Essay #5542). No one is sure how he got there, but seals can eat freshwater fish. However, dogs and seals don't mix.

Jim recalls both Spot and Tar (Spot's offspring) would stand on the dock barking at the seal, and

Butch the seal would come up and slap his flippers on the water. Barking at a seal from the dock is one thing, but if the dogs fell in the water, they rushed out as fast as they could. Seals have the advantage in the water, and the dogs did not want any encounters. So they stayed on the dock— except for one memorable incident.

One summer when the family was having an outdoor picnic, the chicken for dinner was left unattended on a table. When Dick went to barbecue the chicken, he saw Spot just finishing the last of it. Jim recalls his father—who rarely lost his temper—being so mad that he chased Spot to the dock. Then Spot was so scared that he jumped into the lake and started swimming to the other side two miles away. This was really unusual, Jim says, because Spot feared the seal so much he never swam. Dick finally had to use the boat to rescue the dog.

Not too long after they moved in, Lou and Dick wanted to go out for an evening. The house was still not completely done, and as the evening went on, it got colder. The babysitter decided to build a fire in the fireplace to take off the chill. Suddenly, the house filled up with smoke! Fortunately, a neighbor came over and showed her how to open the damper, and they opened the door and got rid of the smoke.

Family vacations were precious times together for the family. But with five children vacations could also be a bit of a challenge. One year, the family rented a houseboat to cruise in the San Juan Islands. The houseboat had two parallel engines. Suddenly, both engines gave out, and they were stranded in one of the many channels in the islands. They were finally rescued and towed to a nearby marina.

Another time, on another boating trip, Dick started the cruise and then eventually became tired. Wanting to take a nap, he turned the steering over to Lou. When he woke up, he discovered they were lost! Lou had turned left instead of right, and it took Dick a long time to figure out where they were and how to get back to where they should be.

In 1967, both John and Jim joined Dick on the Trans-Canadian train ride to Expo 67 in Montreal. And in the early 1970s John, Jim, and Dick were part of a weeklong scouting trip to the Bowron Lakes Provincial Park in British Columbia.

Lou went on to have a career of her own. She applied for a job as soon as their youngest son Doug took his first step on a school bus. She was offered a job at what was then Pacific Northwest Bell as a group chief operator.

Dick knew she was interested in a job, but he thought, *"Who is going to hire a woman with five kids?"*

Within two years, Lou was a chief operator manager, directly supervising 100 operators and four to five group chief operators. As Lou says, *"It was easy after raising five children."* She retired in 1979, after 10 years.

Jim recalls that once she started her job, she would leave early in the morning to get to Seattle on time for work. Their grandmother, Elsie—Dick's mother—would come over at three every afternoon to meet the kids after school and prepare dinner for everyone.

At a family gathering during Christmas 2010, Dick asked the 16 people around the table to take no more than three minutes to talk about one of their fondest memories. When it came to Lou, Dick was so touched to hear that she still remembered meeting him at Seabeck and watching him play volleyball.

FAMILY LIFE

As of August 2013, Dick and Lou have been married for 58 years.

Professionally, at this writing, John, the eldest son, has a master's degree in information technology from the University of Oregon and is director of technology at *Dick's* Drive-In Restaurants. John has a son Alex from a previous marriage, and a grandson, Aiden Glen Thomas Spady. John and his wife Tatyana Tsyrlina-Spady live in Seattle where John is the social/civic entrepreneur for the Dick Spady Legacy Projects (on Twitter @jspady).

Jim is Vice President, CEO, and Corporate Legal Counsel at *Dick's.* He has a business and economics degree from Arizona State University and a law degree from the University of Washington. He and his wife Fawn have two children—Jasmine (now married to David Donovan) and a son, Saul. Jim and Fawn were blessed with their first grandchild (James Richard Donovan) in 2013.

Their third son, Walt, is Vice President and CFO at *Dick's,* and has a bachelor's degree in physics and math from the University of Oregon. He is married to Nan Avant-Spady.

Carol, Dick and Lou's only daughter, graduated from Western Washington University in Bellingham with a degree in education. She lives in Maine with her son, Lucas James DesPres. Carol received her Master's degree in Social Work and is a dedicated therapist and counselor for her community.

Doug, their youngest child, has a degree in zoology, and is CEO of his own company—Doug's Boats/RV and Outdoor in Woodinville, started in 1987. Together with his wife Julie they have two children: Chad, a graduate of Burlington High School and a student at Western Washington University, and Danielle, who attends Annie Wright Schools in Tacoma.

Dick has always been engaged in the community. After they moved to Bellevue, Dick was one of the founding board members of the Bellevue/Overlake Rotary Club in District 5030. This Rotary eventually sponsored one of the first Rotaries in the Soviet Union—thus introducing the concept of "service above self" to an entirely new continent.

Lou and Dick's commitment to each other and the community lives on in their children. Their commitment to quality lives on in the restaurants, extensive community interests, and in the respect and generous benefits they provide their employees.

The Dick Spady story is one of a life driven by vision and values, filled with love for family, and respect for employees and customers who made his vision succeed. He has been recognized and honored by the Seattle community that embraced his business and praised him for giving back to the community what he himself had been given. Dick's bottom line is an undying passion to give the public the voice they deserve. He believes that every voice matters, whether it is *Dick's* customers or the voting public.

Ultimately, he would probably say, *"We are only as successful as the satisfaction of those we serve."*

Kathleen L. O'Connor is a writer living in Seattle, Washington, who was commissioned by John Spady to tell Dick's story.

Appendices

1. Dick's Philosophy of Business

Our Business Philosophy
By Dick Spady, President, *Dick's* Drive-In Restaurants, Inc.
(June 11, 2010)

Since January 1954 we have tried always to do our best to serve high quality food, with fast service, at low prices. These are the three foundations on which the Fast Food industry was built. However, our broader business philosophy is built on four key duties.

THE FIRST RESPONSIBILITY OF A BUSINESS IS TO ITSELF; *it must survive.* Business is all about filling human needs. If one can find a human need—any human need—and fill it, one can have a business be it big or small. A business must thrive—its income must be greater than its expenses, i.e., it must make a "profit." If it can't make a profit, it cannot even take care of itself let alone anyone else.

THE SECOND RESPONSIBILITY OF A SUCCESSFUL BUSINESS IS TO TREAT ITS EMPLOYEES AND SUPPLIERS FAIRLY—both are needed in order to deliver goods and services to **customers**, i.e., to the *people—the ultimate benefactors of a successful business.* In this regard *Dick's* provides the highest pay rate in our industry at $9.50/hour to start and $10.00/hour after certain basic skills are learned, which normally takes 90 days. These are well above minimum wage. Employees working at least 24 hours per week also get 100% employer-paid medical insurance and are eligible to receive a four-year, $18,000 college scholarship after just six months if they continue to work at least 20 hours per week. We also pay our employees up to four hours extra per month for volunteering at any local charity and offer a 401(K) retirement plan with a 50% match.

THE THIRD RESPONSIBILITY OF A BUSINESS IS TO ITS IMMEDIATE COMMUNITY to help it in whatever way it can because as the community goes so goes a business. In this regard *Dick's* conducts a "Change for Charity" program in which customers contribute their spare change to the problem of Seattle homelessness through donations to Operation Nightwatch, FareStart, Rotary Youth Foundation and other charitable groups. The program has generated over $390,000 since 1999. We have also made significant contributions in support of the Wallingford Boys and Girls Club for both its capital campaign and its educational "Let's Talk" programming services for young adults in King County and nationwide.

THE FINAL RESPONSIBILITY OF A SUCCESSFUL BUSINESS IS TO THE COMMON GOOD TO BUILD TOWARD A SUSTAINABLE COMMUNITY. If a business is still successful economically at this point, we believe its final responsibility is to the common good. Not just to provide money to the community, which it should do—but also *giving of one's time—both employees and owners*. Why? Because these individuals, as a part of a successful business, have more time than most others to think, plan, and organize *civilization building*.

Ultimately our task is ***civilization building***—a task at a level above politics and above economics—a task where every individual on earth is fully employed from birth to death. Even if a person has the humblest of circumstances, he and she always have their greatest spiritual gift of being alive and human—their ability to think—*including their God-given spiritual gift to discern right from wrong, i.e., ethics*. Jacob Bronowski, author of *The Ascent of Man, 1973,* states it most eloquently, "Science is the world of what is, ethics is the world of what ought to be." He goes on to ask, "We measure the world of science all the time. Why can't we measure the world of what ought to be?" The answer is **yes we can *if citizens are enabled*** by their political, economic, community, and religious leaders *to be heard*. Freedom of speech, to peaceably assemble, and to petition are hollow rights if people feel unable to be heard.

A sustainable dialogue is a precursor to a sustainable community. Bronowski warned us: "[There are those who are] in love with the aristocracy of the intellect. And that is a belief that can only destroy the civilization that we know. If we are anything, we must be a democracy of the intellect. We must not perish by the distance between people and government, between people and power."

The human race is on the verge of a major discovery in social science comparable to the printing press and the computer. Most of the knowledge in the world is in books and computer databanks. *Wisdom*, however, is something subtly different from knowledge. Wisdom is more a process of taking knowledge and expertise and applying or proposing that it be applied to the problems faced by people in their world. *Wisdom is in the minds of people walking the earth, and we have to learn how to reach it.*

Thank you again for the opportunity to speak with you today about *Dick's* Drive-In Restaurants. We appreciate the opportunity given to us to serve Seattle, King County, our state, our nation, and the world. May your opportunities to serve be even greater.

Sincerely,

Dick Spady, President and Co-Founder
Dick's Drive-In Restaurants, Inc.

DicksDriveIn.com CommunityForumsNetwork.org NatDialogue.org AIForums.org

2. Dick's Employee Benefits

Employment - Dick's Drive-In

For more information call 206-634-0300

Health and Dental Benefits
Dick's offers 100% employer-paid health insurance and employer-subsidized dental insurance to every employee who works at least 24 hours per week (which amounts to over 75% of our employees.)

Educational Scholarships
College, vocational/self-improvement scholarships up to $22,000 over 4 years to employees working 20 hours per week for at least six months and continuing to work at least 20 hours per week while attending school. For more information about how to qualify and apply visit www.DicksDriveIn.com/scholarship.

Childcare Assistance
As an extension of our Scholarship Program, childcare assistance of between $3,000-$8,000 per year is available to employees working 20 hours per week for at least six months -- and continuing to work at least 20 hours per week while receiving

childcare assistance. If an employee doesn't use any or all of their available scholarship funds for tuition, they can use it for childcare.

Paid Community Service

We feel it is important for our employees to get involved in our community. Our community service benefit encourages employees to help local charities. *Dick's* will pay volunteer-employee's their regular hourly wage for up to 4 hours per month of volunteer time.

Higher Wages

We pay employees at least $10.25 per hour to start (higher than the amount typically paid by *Dick's* competitors and well above the current minimum wage). Merit raises can increase your hourly wage to $10.75 per hour within three months. Shift Managers earn up to $5.00 per hour over-and-above their base wage. Store Managers earn considerably more.

Dick's is Committed to Our Employees

As far as we know, no other fast food restaurant in the Seattle area even comes close to Dick's in its commitment to employees. *Dick's* employees earn this recognition by working harder to give every *Dick's* customer the fastest service around, without ever compromising Dick's historic commitment to quality and the highest levels of health and sanitation. Dick's employees are probably the most loyal in the industry. Almost one-third of all Dick's employees have worked for the company for 2 years or more. Although Dick's commitment to its employees, like Dick's commitment to quality food, costs more in the short-run, it has been an excellent long-run strategy by giving both customers and employees extra value.

3. Red and Rover: Brian Bassett Comic Strip

4. Senate Resolution 1993-8636

WASHINGTON STATE SENATE

SENATE RESOLUTION
8696

By Senators Esser, Jacobsen, Kohl-Welles, Johnson, Fraser and McAuliffe

WHEREAS, Dick Spady co-founded *Dick's* Drive-in Restaurants; and

WHEREAS, *Dick's* Drive-in Restaurants have served the greater Seattle community for 50 years since its opening day on January 28, 1954; and

WHEREAS, The people of the State of Washington have enjoyed countless numbers of *Dick's* mouth-watering hamburgers, fresh fries, and hand-dipped shakes served by the hands of a friendly staff; and

WHEREAS, *Dick's* has maintained its principles of quality food and customer service at a low price throughout its 50 years and expansion to five restaurants; and

WHEREAS, *Dick's* gives back to the greater Seattle community through its outstanding consideration for its 120 employees, as evidenced by the company's high wages, frequent pay raises, health insurance benefits, paid time off for community service, subsidized day care, and $12,000 college scholarships; and

WHEREAS, Customers have come to know *Dick's* Drive-in Restaurant as a place to go to experience camaraderie, spark up a romance, and feel a sense of community among workers and customers alike; and

WHEREAS, Apart from his business, Dick Spady has given back to the community through his work with the Forum Foundation to create a "symbolic dialogue" between citizens and elected officials; and

WHEREAS, Dick Spady has worked to incorporate this symbolic dialogue in all his interpersonal relations, from his work with his staff and suppliers to his work with state legislators;

NOW, THEREFORE, BE IT RESOLVED, That the Washington State Senate officially recognize Dick Spady for his service to the greater Seattle community as a small business owner and community activist on the 50th anniversary of *Dick's* Drive-in Restaurant's opening day; and

BE IT FURTHER RESOLVED, That the Washington State Senate does hereby celebrate January 28, 2004, *Dick's* Drive-in Appreciation Day, and wishes the "*Dick's* family" a happy 50th anniversary.

I, Milton H. Doumit, Jr., Secretary of the Senate,
do hereby certify that this is a true and
correct copy of Senate Resolution 8696,
adopted by the Senate
January 28, 2004

MILTON H. DOUMIT, JR.
Secretary of the Senate

5. Honorary Doctorate

Let all to whom these presents come know that in recognition of his contributions to Russian democratic institutions and his efforts on behalf of Russian higher education,

THE UNIVERSITY OF RUSSIA'S ACADEMY OF EDUCATION

does this day of June 2, 2003, confer upon

RICHARD SPADY

the degree of Doctor of Humane Letters, with all the rights and privileges thereunto pertaining.

Boris Bim-Bad, President

6. Awards and Honors

The many honors and awards received both by Dick Spady and Dick's Drive-In speak volumes about the my family's care and concern for the community (where "community" for my father passes simultaneously through every point from "local" to "international".) The following is not a comprehensive list of the awards and appointments accepted by my father but they are ones that he is especially thankful for. -John Spady

1965-1968, Seattle District Lay Leader, The United Methodist Church

1993, Earl Award, from the World Network of Religious Futurists and associated with the World Future Society, named after the late Dr. Earl D.C. Brewer (d. 1993), director of the Center for Religious Research and professor emeritus of religion and society at Emory University. Brewer was a pioneer of the 20th century who placed the study of religion in a futures context.

2001, Bishop's Award, Pacific Northwest Annual Conference of the United Methodist Church. Presented by Bishop Elias Galvan "for working tirelessly on behalf of Methodism and democratic principles in this country and abroad, and for the humanitarian model he set as an employer for *Dick's* Drive-In Restaurants."

2001 Hero of the Homeless Award from Operation Nightwatch, Seattle.

2003, Doctor of Humanities Letters, D.Litt., from the University of Russia's Academy of Education, "for contributions to Russian democracy and higher education."

2005, Business of the Year Award with Civic Recognition from the Municipal League of King County

2006, Hero Award from Washington Dollars for Scholars

2006, National Community Service Award from the Daughters of the American Revolution

2007, Sri Sri Ravi Shankar Award for Uplifting Human Values, from The Art of Living Foundation (photo included herein)

2007-2009, appointed Citizen Councilor Coordinator of the Countywide Community Forums by the King County Auditor, reappointed **Coordinator Emeritus in 2010**

2008, Bruce Briggs Community Service Award, from the Association of Washington Business

2012, Esquire Magazine, *Most Life-Changing Burger Joint,* in a national online opinion poll

7. Mayor's Proclamation

City of Seattle

PROCLAMATION

WHEREAS,   For over 58 years Dick's commitment has been to a high quality product and low prices, alongside investments in the communities where the restaurant does business; and

WHEREAS,   Dick's Drive-In has provided the highest wages and benefits in its industry, including $10 per hour to start, 100 percent employer-paid health insurance premiums, a $22,000 college scholarship plan, paid time off for community service, and a 401(k) plan with a 50 percent employer match; and

WHEREAS,   Over the past 20 years, Dick's Drive-In employee scholarship program has paid out over $1.2 million; and

WHEREAS,   Along with their customers' 'Change for Charity' donations, Dick's Drive-In has provided over $1 million to support local homeless charities, disaster relief efforts around the world, and public engagement efforts in Seattle, King County, and now statewide; and

WHEREAS,   Dick's Drive-In has the lowest turnover rates in the fast food industry and supports 180 local jobs, expanding by more than 40 employees since 2009; and

WHEREAS,   Dick's Drive-In creates a sense of place for Seattleites - from going with your parents to your grad night to your last stop on the way home;

NOW, THEREFORE, I, MIKE MCGINN, Mayor of the City of Seattle, do hereby proclaim July 9, 2012, to be

DICKS DRIVE-IN DAY

in Seattle, and I encourage all citizens to join me in recognizing this extraordinary company for their outstanding contributions to our community.

MIKE MCGINN
Mayor

Made in the USA
Charleston, SC
24 April 2015